Hypnotherapy and Hypnosis

Edited by Cengiz Mordeniz

Published in London, United Kingdom

IntechOpen

Supporting open minds since 2005

Hypnotherapy and Hypnosis
http://dx.doi.org/10.5772/intechopen.83045
Edited by Cengiz Mordeniz

Contributors
Hudu Garba Mikail, Mohammed Mamman, Elizabeth Brooker, Arnoldo Tellez, Rashit Tukaev, Tal Dotan Ben-Soussan, Patrizio Paoletti, Joseph Glicksohn, Cengiz Mordeniz, Arturo Valdez, Teresa Sánchez-Jáuregui

First published in London, United Kingdom, 2020 by IntechOpen
IntechOpen is the global imprint of INTECHOPEN LIMITED, registered in England and Wales, registration number: 11086078, 5 Princes Gate Court, London, SW7 2QJ, United Kingdom
Printed in Croatia

British Library Cataloguing-in-Publication Data
A catalogue record for this book is available from the British Library

Additional hard and PDF copies can be obtained from orders@intechopen.com

Hypnotherapy and Hypnosis
Edited by Cengiz Mordeniz
p. cm.
Print ISBN 978-1-83962-764-4
Online ISBN 978-1-83962-765-1
eBook (PDF) ISBN 978-1-83962-766-8

For EU product safety concerns:
IN TECH d.o.o., Prolaz Marije Krucifikse Kozulić 3, 51000 Rijeka, Croatia, info@intechopen.com or visit our website at intechopen.com.

Meet the editor

Cengiz Mordeniz, is an associate professor at the Department of Anesthesiology and Intensive Care and Pain Medicine at Namık Kemal University, Turkey. He is the founder of the Traditional and Complementary Medical Center at The University Hospital where he also works. He obtained specialization in Anesthesiology and Intensive Care at Istanbul University and a master's degree in Forensic Medicine and Clinical Deontology at Acibadem University, Turkey. He pursued research and clinical practice at Rigs Hospitalet, Denmark; Heidelberg and Giessen Universities, Germany; and Plovdiv University, Bulgaria. He was trained at Moscow Quantum Medicine Academy, Russia, and School of Advanced International Studies on Applied Theoretical and Non-Linear Methodologies of Physics, Italy. He completed the Clinical Research Program at Harvard University. He is a member of HeartMath Institute

Contents

Preface

History of hypnosis goes as far back as that of sorcery, magic, and medicine; people have been entering hypnotic-type trances for thousands of years through different forms of meditation in religions of many cultures.

Scientific history of hypnosis, however, only began in the eighteenth century with Franz Mermer, a German physician who used hypnosis to treat patients, as he believed that hypnosis was a supernatural force that flowed from the hypnotist into the subject.

In the nineteenth century, James Braid, a Scottish surgeon, coined the terms *hypnotism* and *hypnosis* after the Greek god of sleep, Hypnos. In the following years, European research demonstrated that hypnosis involved no physical forces or physiological processes, but was merely a combination of psychologically mediated responses to suggestions.

Austrian physician Sigmund Freud was among many who studied hypnosis. He initially used it as a method to help neurotics to recall disturbing memories that they might have forgotten, but later discarded hypnosis in favor of free association.

Hypnosis is a special conscious state characterized by increased receptiveness and awareness. The hypnotist can provoke a variety of psychological, sensory, and motor responses via appropriate suggestions. These suggestions can cause a subject to act as deaf, blind, paralyzed, hallucinated, delusional, amnesic, or impervious to pain or other stimuli. Hypnotized subjects may react in an uncritical and automatic fashion and be inclined to see, feel, smell, and perceive according to the hypnotist's suggestions. The hypnotic changes are not only sensory but also related to the subject's memory and awareness even in extension to the subsequent post-hypnotical activities.

The use of hypnosis in medicine is called medical hypnotherapy and can be efficient in many conditions such as chronic pain, anxiety, mood disorders, and habit changes as in smoking cessation. In many cases, hypnotherapy is superior to other non-pharmacological interventions in providing analgesia, reducing stress, relieving anxiety, and improving sleep and behaviors.

Hypnotherapy can be tailored to different treatment methods, such as cognitive-behavioral therapy. Patients can become more empowered by learning to hypnotize themselves at home to reduce chronic pain, improve sleep, or alleviate some symptoms of depression or anxiety. Cognitive hypnotherapy refers to an empirically based approach using cognitive-behavioral therapy to achieve an integrative approach to clinical hypnosis.

This book reevaluates hypnosis and hypnotherapy in the light of modern brain sciences findings, explaining the scientific mechanism of hypnosis and assessing the techniques used in clinical and medical practice. The aim of this book is to guide professionals in integrating hypnotherapy into conventional evidence-based medicine.

Dr. Cengiz Mordeniz
Associate Professor,
Medical Faculty,
Tekirdag Namik Kemal University,
Tekirdag, Turkey

Section 1

The Role of Hypnosis in Modern Medical Practice

Chapter 1

Hypnosis and Hypnotherapy: Emerging of Science-Based Hypnosis

Cengiz Mordeniz

Abstract

Hypnosis, which has been used for centuries in different forms, has to be reevaluated in the light of modern medicine and science by biological, psychological, sociological and spiritual approach. Hypnosis has been regaining its popularity in the trend of personalized and holistic medicine without any drug, injection or side effects.

Keywords: hypnosis, dissociation, absorption, fantasy proneness, imaginative capabilities, eye-movement techniques, expectancies, imaginative involvement, rapport, resonance

1. Definition

Hypnosis is an agreement of a social interaction between a subject (designated as patient) and the hypnotist (healthcare professional) who suggests imaginative experiences to change sensation, cognition, affect, mood, or behavior in perception, memory, and voluntary control of action. Hypnosis promotes relaxation, enhances imagery to therapeutically recover forgotten incidents [1].

2. History of hypnosis

In mythology, Hypnos (Somnus, in Latin) is the personification of sleep who lived with his twin brother, Thanatos (Θάνατος, "death personified") in a dark under world cave on Lemnos island (according to Homer or Book XI of Ovid's Metamorphoses) without any light from the sun or the moon; where flowed Lethe, the river of forgetfulness. His parents were Nyx (Νύξ, night) and Erebus (darkness), and he married with, Pasithea, the goddess of marriage and birth and the deity of hallucination and relaxation. Their sons called Oneiroi (dreams) were bringers of dreams. Among them Morpheus, brought human dreams; Icelus, animal dreams; and Phantasus, dreams of inanimate things. A bronze head of Hypnos is in British Museum in London (**Figure 1**). The English word "hypnosis" refers to a person put into a sleep-like state (hypnos "sleep" + –osis "condition"). Hypnosis was used in the temples of Aesculapius, the God of Medicine, where priests advised patients during their sleep as gods talking to them in their dreams. Etymologically speaking, Somnus, Latin word for sleep, is the source of many English words such as insomnia (sleeplessness), somnolent (sleepy), hypersomnia (excessive sleep), and hypnotics(sleep inducing drugs) among many others [3].

Figure 1.
Hypnos and thanatos carrying the body of sarpedon from the battlefield of Troy. Detail from an Attic white-ground lekythos, ca. 440 BC [2].

Mesmer, founder of modern hypnosis, considered animal magnetism, an invisible magnetic fluid in all living things, as the cause of illness, which could be treated by manipulating with his hands through hypnosis (**Figure 2**). Although mesmerism was therapeutically effective, a scientific commission of inquiry attributed the effects of hypnosis to imagination in France in 1784 [5].

The Marquis de Puységur, who experimented with animal magnetism, put a peasant, into a sleep-like-state, a "sleep of senses," after which he could not recall his responses to the suggestions during his sleep. A will to direct an organic power unites the magnetizer with the subject. Puységur actually evoked the latent capacity of the subject's mental and emotional state by paying attention and showing a kind

DOI: http://dx.doi.org/10.5772/intechopen.94089

Figure 2.
Drawing room scene with many people sitting and standing around a large table; a man on a crutch has an iron band wrapped around his ankle; others in the group are holding bands similarly; to the left, a man has hypnotized a woman [4].

of benevolent love. This was the beginning of hypnosis. Puységur noted significant responses from his subject:

a. sleep-waking state, that he called "magnetic sleep" or "magnetic somnambulism," resembled natural sleep-walking condition,

b. rapport, a special connection with the magnetizer,

c. suggestibility, heightened capacity to imagine vividly,

d. amnesia in waking state for the events occurred in the state of magnetic sleep,

e. ability to read the thoughts of the magnetizer, and diagnose the subject's own illness,

f. change in the personality of the magnetic subject, with increased alertness and self-confidence [6].

Freud also used hypnosis considering as hysterical reactions to traumatic experiences in childhood and a mobilization of transference phenomena. Hypnotic techniques helped the soldiers to alleviate the effects of traumatic experiences during World War II and treat "traumatic neuroses" [7].

By second half of the 19th century, Braid coined the term hypnotism and Erickson promoted new approaches to psychotherapy using hypnosis through storytelling [8].

3. Neurophysiology and hypnosis

Hypnotic modulation of suffering provokes changes in the anterior cingulate cortex, leaving primary sensory cortex unaffected. Hypnotic modulation of color perception draining or adding color to a stimulus, real or hallucinated, activates the fusiform color area and the inferior temporal region of cerebral cortex with clearer effects in the left cerebral hemisphere than the right. The activation in the left fusiform area is only affected during hypnosis while the right fusiform activation is affected in both hypnotic and control condition. fMRI (functional magnetic resonance imaging) shows heightened activity in the prefrontal cortex. The hypnotized people produce activity in the visual cortex to hallucinate an image. Hypnotic alteration of perception, involves top-down resetting of the intensity of perceptual response, rather than post perception processing changes. There is a decrease in the activity of the dorsal anterior cingulate (dACC) and an increase in connections between the dorsolateral prefrontal cortex and the insula connections between the dorsolateral prefrontal cortex and the default mode network including medial prefrontal and posterior cingulate cortex also weaken) [9, 10].

Hypnotizability is a stable trait and assessed using scales based on the behavioral response of the person in a social context which is correlated with objective physiological responses. Brain activity and plasticity changes in hypnosis measured by functional magnetic resonance imaging (fMRI), positron-emission-tomography (PET) and electroencephalography (EEG) showed that hypnosis inhibits the reaction of the fear circuitry structures. Frontal and cingulate cortices are most linked to hypnotic responding [11].

Frontal functions have a central role in hypnotic responding. In the first phase of hypnosis, during the induction, the subject's attention on an object stimulates fronto-limbic structures, which are inhibited and/or dissociated in the second phase. In the third phase, right-sided temporo-posterior regions are stimulated. In response to hypnosis, the fronto-cortical activity is reduced and the dorsolateral prefrontal cortex structures are dissociated and the cingulate activity increases or decreases depending on the suggestions. Hypnotic responding demonstrates greater dominance in the right hemisphere than left hemisphere processing, associated with cognitive activities while no difference is found in hypnotizability between left and right hemisphere lesions. *Highs have significantly larger rostrum than lows. Hypnosis influences the connectivity between brain regions. The connectivity is decreased between frontal midline areas and left lateral scalp sites in highs while increased between left temporal and right occipital areas in lows.* Areas and type of activity changes in the brain depend on the suggestions, rather than hypnosis per se. Highs are more prone to hypnotic suggestions by higher levels of theta activity and structural connectivity between left and right hemisphere frontal areas. Reducing frontal activity increases the response to hypnotic suggestions and not a general hypnotic responsivity [12–27].

4. Clinical applications

Hypnosis is performed to relieve pain in abdominal, breast, cardiac, genitourinary and orthopedic surgery. Hypnosis is a powerful means of altering pain, anxiety, and various somatic functions, and recovering forgotten incidents. Hypnosis is found efficient in cancer care even in bone cancer, leukemia, and lymphoma, specifically focused on treatment-induced and conditioned anticipatory nausea/vomiting, pain, anxiety/distress, and hot flashes to manage cancer-related pain, anxiety, fear, lack of appetite. Potential method to manage side effects associated with cancer and cancer treatment.

Patients receiving local anesthetic plus hypnosis experience less anticipatory procedure-related anxiety, and demonstrate less behavioral distress. Hypnosis-based interventions for cancer pain have significant pain reduction, especially when used in combination with other psychosocial-behavioral techniques and supportive-group therapy. Beneficial effects of hypnosis to treat anxiety and distress among cancer patients remained for at least 3 months' post-intervention, without any adverse effect, relative to an educational intervention controlling the effects of time, therapist attention, and participation from pediatric to geriatric patients, among both sexes. Hypnosis delivered by a therapist is found more effective than self-hypnosis. Self-hypnosis training represents a rapid, cost-effective, nonaddictive, safe and efficacious treatment for anxiety prior to tests, surgery and medical procedures and anxiety-related disorders and psychological disorders such as stress, ego strengthening, unipolar depression, smoking cessation, weight loss, and rehabilitation. The hypnotic intervention is twice less expensive than the standard sedation procedure [28–32].

5. Hypnosis associated phenomena

5.1 Suggestion phenomena

- Suggestibility,

Hypnotic suggestibility relies on different cognitive processes. Sensory Suggestibility requires the ability to imagine a non-existent, but suggested, sensation. Methods that do not rely on trance, but heighten suggestibility are reflex conditioning, abstract conditioning, repetitive sensory stimulation, use of imagination, and misdirection of attention.

- primary suggestibility, direct suggestions for facilitation and inhibition of motor activity,

- secondary suggestibility, implied suggestions for sensory/perceptual changes;

- tertiary suggestibility, attitude changes in response to persuasive communications;

- interrogative suggestibility, occurs following misleading post-event information; or placebo response.

Posthypnotic suggestion: the subject takes the posthypnotic suggestion as a conscious act and continues responding to suggestions delivered in hypnosis even after the termination of hypnosis. The subject can receive and carry out posthypnotic suggestions. Periodic reinforcement makes the posthypnotic suggestions more effective because the behavior is experienced automatically without involvement of executive awareness of this activity.

5.2 Ideosensory response phenomena

Hallucination: "hallucination" is a vivid visual ideosensory response, experiencing something that is not actually happening but feeling as it were happening. Hallucination can be used for aversion therapy, to stop a habit such as smoking, nail biting etc. The person can hallucinate any of the senses. When the subject perceives a specific object that is not actually present in the stimulus environment experience; it is called positive ideosensory response and positive hallucination. If he/she fails to perceive a specific object that is present in the stimulus environment, it is called negative ideosensory response and negative hallucination.

Anesthesia is reduction or loss of any sensory modality, such as blindness, deafness, anosmia, analgesia, or tactile anesthesia. Self -generated pain control can be recreated using hypnotic suggestion for various conditions such as headache and dystonia. Surgery can be performed using only hypnotic anesthesia for pain management without any drug. Not everybody can achieve the depth of trance required for surgical work, but they can become suggestible enough to produce numbness in hand referred as "glove anesthesia," then "transferred" by touch wherever needed. Numbness of any part of the body can occur spontaneously so profoundly that needles can be inserted into the body without discomfort. If the hypnotist tells to the subject to reduce its perception through sensation of tingling and numbness, with decreased activity of somatosensory dorsal anterior cingulate cortex (dACC). Hypno-analgesia cannot be reversed by naloxone, an opiate receptor blocker.

5.3 Ideomotor phenomena

Ideomotor responses refer to motor phenomena of muscles responding instantaneously to thoughts and feelings, a movement in response to an idea. The subject moves in response to a suggestion given during hypnosis.

Catalepsy: involuntary tonicity, rigidity or immobility of muscles. It can happen naturally in a fight, flight or freeze state where the body is stuck in place even though the mind tells to move. It can be used in induction/deepening process (with an eye catalepsy/eye lock test) during eyeball catalepsy. Psychogenic sexual issues such as erectile dysfunction or insomniacs who move around too much in their sleep can be relieved by hypnotic catalepsy.

Automatic Writing: "Doodling" is the manifestation of automatic writing and answering to completely different questions without any conscious effort while talking or listening. Then, the subject can interpret what was written in hypnosis.

5.4 Memory phenomena

The hypnotic state of the brain activity is a sort of functional amnesia, a reversible dissociation between implicit and explicit memory (post hypnotic amnesia (PHA)).

Amnesia refers to the act of forgetting. Spontaneously occurred amnesia indicates deep state of hypnosis known as somnambulism. Amnesia is a temporary result of specific hypnotic suggestions.

Somnambulism: deep stage of hypnosis like sleepwalkers' experience. Hypnotic suggestions become automatic convictions which cannot be recollected by the subject. The hypnotized subject obeys to the directions as awake.

Posthypnotic amnesia, the subject cannot remember events and experiences that he/she lived during hypnosis.

False memory syndrome: Events are processed by the physical brain to become memories accessible by the non-physical mind. A false belief into the mind of another can be instilled.

Cryptomnesia is responsible for past life regression episodes. Invisibly stored information within the brain can be recalled as a result of a stimulus.

Repression: Profound guilt or vulnerability to shame, hate, death, causes to "hide" the event in a time capsule in the mind, so that consciousness is no longer aware of the vulnerability. Repressed memories can lay dormant for years doing nothing for the owner. The conscious mind uses rationalization, as a logical reason for the symptoms associated with the reminiscent event of the original trauma. Repression, a function of the mind's capacity can be triggered by anything within human experience connected to the repressed memory in forming new instinctive behavior patterns relevant to the living environment. Hypnoanalysis resistance means to abort therapy because of a threat to security felt by the subject. The memory is composed of three separate parts– event, physiological reaction, emotional response. Any one or all three can be repressed.

Hypermnesia (Memory Recall): Experiencing heightened recall abilities during hypnosis is known as hypermnesia. It is the act of remembering more than normal (enhanced recall). Since the material can be inaccurate or false, hypnotically recovered memories are not allowed as "evidence" in court cases. The main use for the phenomena of hypermnesia assists in finding lost items and discovering their locations by remembering past events to attain further details. The hypnotherapist will ask the subject to let the mind drift to the last time that he/she saw the item or places to be with it or handling and to remember and say as much about the item.

Regression: the subject just imagines vividly going back to a past event being aware that he/she is not actually there. It is used for phobias that have started during childhood.

Age Regression (Pseudo revivification): The subject relives previous life experiences as if they happened in present. The subject goes to earlier experiences related to the current problem in a present existence.

Pseudo-regression: Instead of identifying the experiences directly, the subject observes the event from another view as if on a television or movie screen.

Revivification: reliving an incident in the present tense as if the subject was there at that time without current knowledge. Revivification requires deeper state of hypnosis and responsiveness to suggestions and can be experienced in the night dreams. Some regress while some others revivify.

Retrogression (Dynamic Regression): Retrogression is a spontaneous age regression with revivification mixed in.

Age Progression: The subject feels living in the future even though remains in present age. Age progression is a mean to predict how a person would react to an event in the future.

5.5 Perception phenomena

Dissociation: to disintegrate the subject from the painful part of the body to get rid of past traumatic events against fears and phobias. The subject would imagine negative situations. It is like watching a memory on a TV screen rather than seeing through the eyes. The dissociation reduces emotional responses of the subject who would go to a happy place to dissociate from what happens here and now.

Depersonalization: The subject ignores his/her own identity, and acts as another person from a new perspective.

Time distortion: The subjective measuring of time can be altered simply by either enjoying or waiting for something in hypnosis. A person feels expansion of time in boredom. Contraction is the opposite like time flying while having fun. For example, a nervous airplane passenger can start to believe to be on the plane for less time or extend the perceived time of someone on a diet.

Future pacing (mental rehearsal): It is kind of visualization where the subject can prepare himself/herself for success and realization of his/her goals by overcoming the potential obstacles through future options [33–35].

6. Theories

A comprehensive theory of hypnosis should cover both cognitive and interpersonal terms. Throughout twentieth century the theories about hypnosis have been between "state" vs. "non-state" theories.

6.1 State theories

Hilgard's Neodissociation Theory entails a division in consciousness.

6.1.1 Dissociated control theory (DCT)

DCT claims that normally driving habitual behaviors can be influenced outside of conscious awareness without executive control. According to Ego-state theorists, clinicians can promote behavioral change by hypnosis, and have conversations with different ego states.

6.1.2 Dissociated-experience theory

High hypnotizables respond voluntarily dissociated from conscious awareness. *The school of* Gerald Brassine *of Belgium has considered hypnosis not only a question of words nor the result of suggestion, but the product of the use of imagery or memories of the person, having a lot of implicit consequences and practical attitudes in the practice, and being natural product of many different things including choc (trauma) days dreaming and psychotherapeutic hypnosis. The hypnotic relationship would develop more easily if the therapist demonstrates that the patient is the only "producer" of this state. In such an equal relationship, the hypnotist becomes a facilitator helping the patient to develop a state of trance, but he/she can reject or come out of it anytime if he/she does not want. This comprehension would facilitate a deep state of hypnosis during which the patient feels as " the boss" of the hypnotic situation, in which he/she does not lose but gains control of his/her emotions and sensations on his/her autonomous nervous system (a psychosomatic control over extremely painful diseases) with the help or assistance of the hypnotist in a cooperative venture. If the therapist understands and acts on this principle at all time, and explains and offers to the patient the knowledge that he/she can produce this phenomenon, the patient would be much more eager to try the proposed possibilities (all classical hypnotic phenomena) and this type of therapist would be much more efficient than any other who just believes that his/her speaking (use of word) and techniques are responsible for the trance of the patient. (It is not far from the Mesmerian conception of animal magnetism or later hypnosis considered as the fruit of the genius suggestions of a therapist). In practice, the emphasis should be on what the patient does and says and not what the therapist says and does.*

In the school of Gerald Brassine *of Belgium, the thought and practice of PTR (Psychotherapie du Trauma Réassociative) is willing to bring the patient in a state of hypnosis by using what is called utilizational hypnosis. It means that the therapist eases the patient to develop and use a trance state in a constant exchange. This comprehension or conceptualization of hypnosis (the result of the use of memory or imaginative capacities) is building an equalitarian form of relationship in which the patient controls his/her sensations and emotions and the therapist supports and indicates to the patient the possibilities of work while keeping in mind that the patient might probably have better ideas on how to solve his/her difficulties. This is called the production of PAAT (in French: Processus Autonomes Auto-Therapeutiques (more or less in English: Autonomous (Self?) Auto-therapeutic Processes).*

Another idea could be the use of the protective dissociations in a concept that implies that the natural apparition of hypnotic phenomena during traumas can be fixed as dissociative reactions turned into symptoms, which can be paradoxically utilized by the therapist to facilitate their eradication as "mental or psychic anesthetics." Directly derived from the concept that hypnosis is not a result of suggestion, this method brings an incredible opportunity to treat the patients rapidly and comfortably in the situation of extreme sufferings and in the treatment of psychosomatic diseases [36].

6.1.3 Gruzelier's neurophysiological theory

High and low hypnotizables are characterized by changes in brain function.

6.2 Non-state theories

6.2.1 Spanos' socio-cognitive theory

Hypnosis is not an altered state of consciousness. Attitudes, beliefs, imaginings, attributions and expectancies form hypnotic experience and outcome depending of the interpretation of the suggestions without active planning and effort. The sociocognitive behavioral model is used together with contemporary cognitive-behavioral psychotherapies focusing the effects of thoughts, beliefs, and imaginings on behavior and emotion.

6.2.2 Kirsch's response expectancy theory

Proposes that subjects have generalized response expectancy in a hypnotic situation and follow the hypnotists's instructions and experience involuntary behaviors attributable to external causes (the hypnotist). Two social factors associated with response to hypnosis: rapport ("therapeutic alliance," "resonance," and "harmony,") and social context are taken in account.

6.3 Integrative/middle-way/neither-one-nor-the-other theories

Cold control theory proposes that the central feature of hypnotic responding is the involuntariness in an actual intentional action.

6.3.1 Brown and Oakley's integrative cognitive theory

Proposes that involuntariness is an attribute to the causes of behavior and suggestions.

An ability-aptitude model considers two factors as the influencing cause of hypnotic response:

1. a latent cognitive ability for hypnotic response

2. the subject's beliefs about his/her hypnotic response

State theories	Non-state theories
Hypnotic inductions produce an altered state of consciousness	Participants respond to suggestion almost as well without hypnosis
Hypnotic "trance" is associated with an altered state of brain function	Participants in hypnosis experiments are actively engaged
Responses to hypnotic suggestions are a result of special processes such as dissociation or other altered states of consciousness	Responses to suggestions are a product of normal psychological processes such as attitudes, expectancies, and motivation
Hypnotizability is remarkably stable over long periods	Suggestibility can be modified with drugs or psychological procedures

Table 1.
State and non-state theories [37].

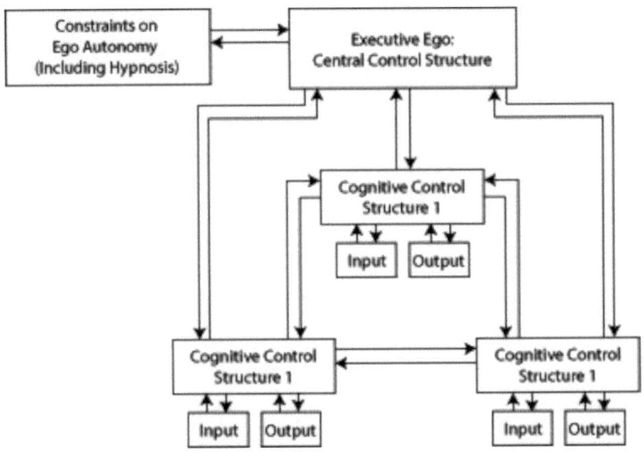

Table 2.
Illustration of Hilgard's neodissociation theory of hypnosis [38].

The social-psychobiological or biopsychosocial model of hypnosis emphasizes the interaction of the hypnotist and the subject, considering their personal characteristics and physiological mechanisms and the contributing role of biological, psychological, and social factors. Hypnotic depth integrates the behavioral aspect (the role of the subject), the phenomenological component (the subjective feeling of trance), and an emotional dimension.

The empathic involvement theory (EIT) of hypnosis proposes a bridging of two incongruent neo dissociative versus socio-cognitive theories of hypnosis. Non-empathic individuals benefit less from hypnosis (**Tables 1–3**) [39–42].

7. Scales

Standardized psychological tests such as the Stanford Hypnotic Susceptibility Scale or the Harvard Group Scale of Hypnotic Susceptibility (SHSS) measure hypnotizability. The Stanford Profile Scales of Hypnotic Susceptibility (SPSHS), in two forms (I and II), evaluates individual strengths and weaknesses. On the individually administered Stanford Scales, each of 12 test suggestions, scored pass-fail, yield a sum score of hypnotizability on a 0-12 scale. The Stanford Hypnotic Susceptibility Scale, Form C (SHSS:C), that contains cognitive suggestions including hallucination and age regression, is the gold standard for measuring hypnotizability.

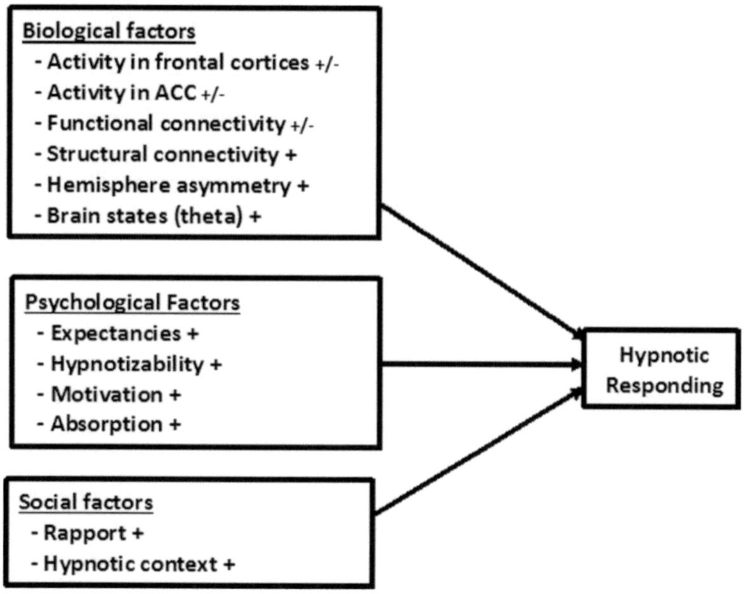

Table 3.
Summary of state of the scientific findings regarding biological, psychological and social factors that contribute to response to hypnosis and hypnotic suggestions. +/– indicates that the factor has demonstrated both positive and negative associations with hypnotic responding: + indicates that the factor has demonstrated mostly positive and consistent associations [43].

The SWASH (Sussex-Waterloo Scale of Hypnotizability) is a 10-item modified Waterloo-Stanford Group C Scale of Hypnotic Suggestibility (WSGC) to reduce screening time and supplement objective scoring. It measures capacity and altering conscious experience. The Dissociative Experiences Scale, a 28-item scale, assesses dissociative experiences. The Tellegen Absorption Scale, a 34-item questionnaire evaluates the capacity of absorption. Dyadic Interactional Harmony questionnaire (DIH) assesses four domains of hypnotist-subject interaction: intimacy, communion, playfulness, and tension. *Valencia Scale of Attitudes and Beliefs Toward Hypnosis scale (VSABTH) considers two reliable measures of attitudes,* response expectancies and emotional distress *toward hypnosis as mediator of hypnotic effects.* PCI-HAP (Phenomenology of Consciousness: Inventory-Hypnotic Assessment Procedure) set out to predict hypnotic depth scores [44–46].

8. Mechanism

The process of hypnosis consists of a hypnotic induction, a deepening procedure, and symptom-specific suggestions. Hypnosis is a state of highly focused attention, with dissociation of thoughts and sensations toward awareness. It is comprised of three components: absorption, dissociation, and suggestibility. Absorption is full involvement in a perceptual, imaginative or ideational experience for self-altering attention. Dissociation is a mental segregation of components of behavior in a dream-like state of being both actor and observer when re-experiencing autobiographical memories in involuntary motor functions or discontinuities in the sensations of one part of the body compared with another. Suggestibility complies with hypnotic instructions. It is not a loss of will but rather a suspension of judgment due to the absorption and effortless self -loss in what is concentrating on. The hypnotized person does not have control over his/her thoughts and actions and follows the suggestions without looking for alternatives and analyzing their context. The principle of hypnosis is to recall traumatic memories and manage their associated affect and physiological responses by reevaluating their meaning in a new perspective. Hypnosis is a set of techniques to fortify concentration, by decreasing the effect of distractions, and increase to change the subject's s thoughts, feelings, behavior, or physiological state. Hypnosis is not psychotherapy. Hypnotic perceptual and cognitive changes the equilibrium between suggestion, expectation, and task instructions [47–49].

A new non-pharmacological technique called virtual reality hypnosis (VRH), combines VR hardware/software and hypnotic induction. In hypnosis, the subject constitutes his own world by the hypnotist's suggestions through absorption and dissociation. Virtual reality hypnosis (VRH) does not depend upon the skill of hypnotist and the openness of the subject. The subjects need less imagination and absorption due to visual and auditory stimuli presented in virtual reality [50–52].

Five psychological factors are most important for the success of hypnosis: hypnotizability, expectancies, motivation, absorptive capacity/fantasy proneness, and attitudes toward hypnosis. The specific type and wording of suggestions influence outcome. Expectancies determine the extent how much the subject believes in the experience and response to the hypnotic intervention. Past experience, current context, and interaction influence expectancies. *The collaborative and affective bond between the hypnotist and the subject is the essential component in hypnosis. The subject's positive response to the contradictory suggestions to his/her previous perception is called countering.* Hypnosis is a change in baseline mental activity. Hypnosis like practices inducing trance states have been used throughout history. Medical hypnosis is applying hypnosis to alleviate somatic symptoms, reduce stress, and influence physiological/biochemical processes. The interactional behavioral and affective synchrony between the child and the parent is highly similar to the relationship between the subject and the hypnotist. Synchrony can occur in the behavioral, emotional, phenomenological, and psycho-physiological variables in both the subject and the hypnotist [53–59].

In psychoanalytic approach to hypnosis, the hypnotist is similar to an authority figure of the subject from his earlier life experience. Frequently punished children would try not to displease the hypnotist and would show high level of dissociation. Negative parental behavior (punishment and overprotection) is related to the phenomenological and emotional dimensions of hypnotic response leading to higher hypnotizability. Parental behavior of the subject influences hypnotic behavior, experiences, and emotional bond with the hypnotist. A warm- supportive parental style provokes more positive feelings toward the hypnotist, whereas cold-punishing parental behavior is correlated to negative feelings about the hypnotist and hypnosis itself. One consistent pattern in females is that maternal punishment predicts only negative affect in hypnosis, while punishing parental behavior in men, predicts both positive and negative responses to hypnosis. Alexithymia, the decreased ability to identify and verbalize someone's own emotions, mediates between parental punishment and fear in hypnosis. Therefore, hypnotherapist should search before the hypnotherapeutic intervention the subject's memories of their parents, which will influence his/her expectations about hypnosis and the hypnotist. Subjects remembering punishing, and/or emotionally unresponsive parents would stay away from the hypnotist even if they know that hypnotherapy would correct the source of the problem. They may feel stress and anxiety in the hypnotic state which can be regulated by the sense of security and mutual trust [60–63].

Mindfulness meditation and hypnosis remain in opposing ways to awareness of intentions. Hypnosis and meditation may be combined as a psychosomatic technique to control mind and body regulation. Phenomenology, and neuropsychology of hypnosis and meditation follow common features:

a. focused attention is the base of induction

b. an intentional control of biologic-somatic activities

c. activation/deactivation of the default modality network and pain neuromatrix [64, 65].

The "mirror neurons" in the human brain provide empathy to sense the intentions of others by observing their behavior and related brain activity. They function as a rapport zone mediating between observing consciousness, the gene expression/protein synthesis cycle, and brain plasticity in hypnotherapy and psychosomatic medicine. (Emerging science recognizes human experience not as disease but as manifestations of individual adaptive self-regulating system) [66].

Tandem hypnotherapy considers the unity of body and mind as a quantum process, since the embryonic period of life. Tandem has two meanings: (1) a multi-seater bicycle, (2) a mosaic word: Touch of Ancient and New generations with a Dialog Experiencing Oneness of Minds (TANDEM). Hypnotherapy, psychodrama, family therapy, Hellinger's systemic-phenomenological approach, and holding-therapy are united in Tandem theory. More than two persons in a physical closeness touching each other take part in therapy: (1) patient(s), (2) one or more co-therapists or antagonists in psychodrama. The therapist takes the responsibility of the tandem of patient(s) and co-therapist(s). Sensory-motor level of development is originated from fetal period of life. In uniting mode of experiencing, object and subject are not seen as different from each other. The most effective stimulus is the physical closeness and touching in intimate situation as a form of body psychotherapy. The psychological factors for hypnosis are hypnotizability, expectations, motivation, absorption/imaginative involvement/fantasy proneness, and attitudes toward hypnosis, and a rapport as social factors lead to "resonance" and "harmony" [67, 68].

Hypnosis and hypnotherapy, which have been experienced for centuries, emerged as new solitary or complementary approach based on science for the wellness of people.

Author details

Cengiz Mordeniz
Tekirdag Namik Kemal University, Turkey

*Address all correspondence to: cengizmorster@gmail.com

References

[1] Kihlstrom, J. F. Hypnosis and the Psychological Unconscious, Editor(s): Howard S. Friedman, Assessment and Therapy, Academic Press, 2001, Pages 215-225, ISBN 9780122678066

[2] https://archive.org/details/historyancientp12bircgoog/page/n1/mode/2up

[3] https://www.greekmythology.com/Other_Gods/Hypnos/hypnos.html

[4] https://harvardmagazine.com/2003/11/hypnosis-heals.html

[5] Hammond DC. A review of the history of hypnosis through the late 19th century. Am J Clin Hypn. 2013;56:174-91. https://doi.org/10.1080/00029157.2013.826172

[6] Crabtree A. 1784: The Marquis de Puységur and the psychological turn in the west. J Hist Behav Sci. 2019;55:199-215. DOI: 10.1002/jhbs.21974

[7] Kluft R.P. (2018) Reconsidering Hypnosis and Psychoanalysis: Toward Creating a Context for Understanding, American Journal of Clinical Hypnosis, 60:3, 201-215, DOI: 10.1080/00029157.2018.1400810

[8] Winter, A. (2000). Mesmerized: Powers of mind in Victorian Britain. Chicago, IL: University of Chicago Press.

[9] Vanhaudenhuyse, S. Laureys, M.-E. Faymonville,. Neurophysiology of hypnosis. Neurophysiologie Clinique/Clinical Neurophysiology,Volume 44, Issue 4,2014, Pages 343-353.

[10] Hoeft, F., Gabrieli, J. D., Whitfield-Gabrieli, S., Haas, B. W., Bammer, R., Menon, V., & Spiegel, D. (2012). Functional brain basis of hypnotizability. Archives of general psychiatry, 69(10), 1064-1072. https://doi.org/10.1001/archgenpsychiatry.2011.2190

[11] Spiegel D, Tranceformations: Hypnosis In Brain And Body Depression And Anxiety 30:342-352 (2013)

[12] Gruzelier JH. Frontal functions, connectivity and neural efficiency underpinning hypnosis and hypnotic susceptibility. Contemporary Hypnosis. 2006;23:15-32.

[13] Dienes Z, Hutton S. Understanding hypnosis metacognitively: rTMS applied to left DLPFC increases hypnotic suggestibility. Cortex. 2013;49(2):386-392.

[14] Kihlstrom JF. Neuro-hypnotism: prospects for hypnosis and neuroscience. Cortex. 2013;49(2):365-374.

[15] Oakley DA, Halligan PW. Psychophysiological foundations of hypnosis and suggestion. In: Lynn SJ, Rhue JW, Kirsch I, editors. Handbook of clinical hypnosis. 2nd ed. Washington, DC: American Psychological Association; 2010. pp. 79-117

[16] Cardeña E, Jonsson P, Terhune DB, Marcusson-Clavertz D. The neurophenomenology of neutral hypnosis. Cortex. 2013;49(2):375-385

[17] Egner T, Jamieson G, Gruzelier J. Hypnosis decouples cognitive control from conflict monitoring processes of the frontal lobe. Neuroimage. 2005;27(4):969-978.

[18] Fingelkurts AA, Kallio S, Revonsuo A. Cortex functional connectivity as a neurophysiological correlate of hypnosis: an EEG case study. Neuropsychologia. 2007;45(7):1452-1462

[19] Pyka M, Burgmer M, Lenzen T, Pioch R, Dannlowski U, Pfleiderer B,

Ewert AW, Konrad C. Brain correlates of hypnotic paralysis—a resting-state fMRI study. Neuroimage. 2011;56:2173-2182

[20] Horton JE, Crawford HJ, Harrington G, Downs JH., 3rd Increased anterior corpus callosum size associated positively with hypnotizability and the ability to control pain. Brain. 2004;127(Pt 8):1741-1747

[21] Moretti D.V. Theta and alpha EEG frequency interplay in subjects with mild cognitive impairment: evidence from EEG, MRI, and SPECT brain modifications, Frontiers in Aging Neuroscience, 7, p. 31 (2015). 10.3389/fnagi.2015.00031

[22] Terhune D.B., Cardeña E. & Lindgren M. Differential frontal-parietal phase synchrony during hypnosis as a function of hypnotic suggestibility Psychophysiology 48, pp. 1444-1447 (2011). 10.1111/j.1469-8986.2011.01211.x

[23] Jamieson G.A. & Burgess A.P. Hypnotic induction is followed by state-like changes in the organization of EEG functional connectivity in the theta and beta frequency bands in high-hypnotically susceptible individuals, Frontiers in Human Neuroscience, 8 (2014).

[24] Deivanayagi S., Manivannan M. & Fernandez P., Spectral analysis of EEG signals during hypnosis, International Journal of Systemics, Cybernetics and Informatics, 4, pp. 75-80 (2007).

[25] Jensen MP. Hypnosis for chronic pain management: Therapist guide. Oxford: Oxford University Press; 2011.

[26] Palsson OS. Hypnosis treatment of gastrointestinal disorders: a comprehensive review of the empirical evidence. Am J Clin Hypn. 2015;58:134-58.

[27] Cramer H, Lauche R, Paul A, Langhorst J, Kümmel S, Dobos GJ. Hypnosis in breast cancer care: a systematic review of randomized controlled trials. Integr Cancer Ther. 2015;14:5-15. https://doi.org/10.1177/1534735414550035

[28] Lisa A. Osborne & Phil Reed (2019) A Review of Hypnotherapy for Overactive Bladder, International Journal of Clinical and Experimental Hypnosis, 67:3, 278-296, DOI: 10.1080/00207144.2019.1612671

[29] Caldwell PHY, Codarini M, Stewart F, Hahn D, Sureshkumar P. Alarm interventions for nocturnal enuresis in children. Cochrane Database of Systematic Reviews 2020, Issue 5. Art. No.: CD002911. DOI: 10.1002/14651858.CD002911.pub3.

[30] Rutten JM, Reitsma JB, Vlieger AM, Benninga MA. Gut-directed hypnotherapy for functional abdominal pain or irritable bowel syndrome in children: a systematic review. Arch Dis Child. 2013;98(4):252-257.

[31] Golden WL. Cognitive hypnotherapy for anxiety disorders. American Journal of Clinical Hypnosis. 2012;54(4):263-274

[32] Assen A. (2012) Cognitive Hypnotherapy for Major Depressive Disorder, American Journal of Clinical Hypnosis, 54:4, 275-293, DOI: 10.1080/00029157.2012.654527

[33] http://johnmongiovi.com/blog/2014/12/01/hypnosis-and-memory

[34] https://www.selfhypnosis.com/hypnotic-phenomena/

[35] http://johnmongiovi.com/blog/2015/09/10/phenomena-of-hypnosis

[36] Brassine G. (2019). Protections dissociatives anesthésiants pour l'hypnothérapie du trauma. Hypnose & therapies breves n° 55:18-26.

[37] Jensen, M. P., Adachi, T., Tomé-Pires, C., Lee, J., Osman, Z. J., & Miró, J. (2015). Mechanisms of hypnosis: toward the development of a biopsychosocial model. The International journal of clinical and experimental hypnosis, 63(1), 34-75. https://doi.org/10.1080/00207144.2014.961875

[38] Woody, E. Z., Sadler, P. (2008). Dissociation theories of hypnosis. In M. R. Nash & A. J. Barnier (eds). The Oxford Handbook of Hypnosis: Theory, Research and Practice. Oxford: Oxford University Press.

[39] Sadler, P., & Woody, E. Z. (2010). Dissociation in hypnosis: Theoretical frameworks and psychotherapeutic implications (PDF). In J. W. Rhue, S. J. Lynn, & I. Kirsch (Eds.), Handbook of clinical hypnosis (2nd ed.) (pp. 151-268). Washington, DC: American Psychological Association.

[40] Lynn, S. J., & Kirsch, I. (2006). Essentials of clinical hypnosis: An evidence-based approach. Washington, DC: American Psychological Association.

[41] Schotte CK, Van Den Bossche B, De Doncker D, Claes S, Cosyns P. A biopsychosocial model as a guide for psychoeducation and treatment of depression. Depress Anxiety. 2006;23(5):312-324

[42] Buckner JD, Heimberg RG, Ecker AH, Vinci C. A biopsychosocial model of social anxiety and substance use. Depression and Anxiety. 2013;30(3):276-284

[43] https://hypnosisandsuggestion.org/

[44] Pam. Stanford Hypnotic Susceptibility Scale, in Psychology Dictionary.org, https://psychologydictionary.org/stanford-hypnotic-susceptibility-scale/

[45] P Lush, G Moga, N McLatchie, Z Dienes, The Sussex-Waterloo Scale of Hypnotizability (SWASH): measuring capacity for altering conscious experience, Neuroscience of Consciousness, Volume 2018, Issue 1, 2018, niy006, https://doi.org/10.1093/nc/niy006

[46] Anlló H, Becchio J, Sackur J. French norms for the Harvard Group Scale of Hypnotic Susceptibility, form A. Int J Clin Exp Hypn 2017;65:241-55

[47] Priftis K, Schiff S, Tikhonoff V et al. Hypnosis meets neuropsychology: simulating visuospatial neglect in healthy participants. Neuropsychologia 2011;49:3346-50

[48] Mallard D, Bryant R. Hypnotic conflict: a brief report. Int J Clin Exp Hypn 2006;54:292-302.

[49] Landry M, Apporchaux K, Raz A. Elucidating unconscious processing with instrumental hypnosis. Front Psychol 2014;5:785

[50] Rousseaux, F., Faymonville, M. E., Nyssen, A. S., Dardenne, N., Ledoux, D., Massion, P. B., & Vanhaudenhuyse, A. (2020). Can hypnosis and virtual reality reduce anxiety, pain and fatigue among patients who undergo cardiac surgery: a randomised controlled trial. Trials, 21(1), 330. https://doi.org/10.1186/s13063-020-4222-6

[51] Enea V, Dafinoiu I, Opriş D, David D. Effects of hypnotic analgesia and virtual reality on the reduction of experimental pain among high and low hypnotizables. Int J Clin Exp Hypn. 2014; 62(3):360-77.

[52] Patterson DR, Jensen MP, Wiechman SA, Sharar SR. Virtual reality hypnosis for pain associated with recovery from physical trauma. Int J Clin Exp Hypn. 2010 Jul; 58(3):288-300.

[53] //doi.org/10.1080/00207144.2014.961875

[54] Wagstaff GF, David D, Kirsch I, Lynn SJ. The cognitive-behavioral model of hypnotherapy. In: Lynn SJ, Rhue JW, Kirsch I, editors. Handbook of clinical hypnosis. 2nd edition ed. Washington, DC: American Psychological Association; 2010. pp. 179-208

[55] Radtke HL, Stam HJ. What happened to the social in contemporary accounts of hypnosis? Contemporary Hypnosis. 2008;25:192-201

[56] Martin DJ, Garske JP, Davis MK. Relation of the therapeutic alliance with outcome and other variables: a meta-analytic review. Journal of Consulting and Clinical Psychology. 2000;68(3):438-450.

[57] Deeley Q, et al. Modulating the default mode network using hypnosis. International Journal of Clinical and Experimental Hypnosis. 2012;60:206-228. doi: 10.1080/00207144.2012.648070

[58] Peter B. Hypnosis. In: Wright JD, editor. International Encyclopedia of the Social & Behavioral Sciences. Second ed. Oxford: Elsevier; 2015. p. 458-64.

[59] Olafur Palsson, Stefanie Twist & Marcia Walker (2019) A National Survey of Clinical Hypnosis Views and Experiences of the Adult Population in the United States, International Journal of Clinical and Experimental Hypnosis, 67:4, 428-448, DOI: 10.1080/00207144.2019.1649538

[60] Bachner-Melman, R., & Lichtenberg, P. (2001). Freud's relevance to hypnosis: A reevaluation. American Journal of Clinical Hypnosis, 44(1), 37-50. doi:10.1080/00029157.2001.10403454

[61] Nash, M. R. (2008). A psychoanalytic theory of hypnosis: A clinically informed approach. In M. R. Nash & A. J. Barnier (Eds.), The Oxford handbook of hypnosis: Theory, research and practice (pp. 201-224). New York, NY: Oxford University Press

[62] Bányai, É. I. (2008b). A hipnózis szociál-pszichobiológiai modellje [The social-psychobiological model of hypnosis]. In É. Bányai & L. Benczúr (Eds.), A hipnózis és a hipnoterápia alapjai [The foundations of hypnosis and hypnotherapy] (pp. 379-445). Budapest, Hungary: ELTE Eötvös Kiadó

[63] Költő, A. (2015). Hypnotic susceptibility and mentalization skills in the context of parental behavior. (Doctoral (PhD) dissertation), Eötvös Loránd University, Budapest, Hungary

[64] Daitch C. (2018) Cognitive Behavioral Therapy, Mindfulness, and Hypnosis as Treatment Methods for Generalized Anxiety Disorder, American Journal of Clinical Hypnosis, 61:1, 57-69, DOI: 10.1080/00029157.2018.1458594

[65] Facco E. (2017) Meditation and Hypnosis: Two Sides of the Same Coin?, International Journal of Clinical and Experimental Hypnosis, 65:2, 169-188, DOI: 10.1080/00207144.2017.1276361

[66] Rossi E.L.Ph.D. & Kathryn *L. Rossi* (2006) The Neuroscience of Observing Consciousness & Mirror Neurons in Therapeutic Hypnosis, American Journal of Clinical Hypnosis, 48:4, 263-278, DOI: 10.1080/00029157.2006.10401533

[67] Vas P J, Császár N. [Body-mind unity in tandem hypnotherapy]. Psychiatr Hung. 2012;27(3):157-64.

[68] Ulrike Halsband & Thomas Gerhard Wolf (2019) Functional Changes in Brain Activity After Hypnosis: Neurobiological Mechanisms and Application to Patients with a Specific Phobia—Limitations and Future Directions, International Journal of Clinical and Experimental Hypnosis, 67:4, 449-474, DOI: 10.1080/00207144.2019.1650551

Chapter 2

Hypnosis and Hypnotherapy: The Role of Traditional Versus Alternative Approach

Mikail Hudu Garba and Mohammed Mamman

Abstract

Hypnosis is a state of mind that is characterized by focused attention and heightened receptivity for suggestions. It is either established by compliance with instructions or achieved naturally; the critical nature of the mind is bypassed during hypnosis and acceptable suggestions are delivered. Misperceptions about hypnosis by clinical practitioners and their clients have been shaped through years of inaccurate but interesting portrayals of hypnosis in books, plays, and movies. Part of the misperceptions is that individuals with seemingly magical powers to manipulate the unsuspecting innocent with their authoritative voice commands and penetrating eyes are depicted as hypnotists. This chapter will review the traditional and conventional approaches used in hypnosis, their advantages and disadvantages as well as where hypnosis is used as a complementary or alternative therapy to the modern day orthodox medicine. Despite the pejorative image display of hypnosis and misconceptions surrounding it, hypnosis still has numerous applications in contemporary medicine. Hypnotherapy conducted by a trained therapist is considered as a complementary or safe alternative to present day orthodox medication for numerous ailments.

Keywords: hypnosis, hypnotherapy, traditional, conventional approaches

1. Introduction

The origin of "hypnosis" is from the Greek word "hypnos," which means "sleep" [1]. Hypnosis is a state of mind that is characterized by focused attention and heightened receptivity for suggestions. It is either established by compliance with instructions or achieved naturally; the critical nature of the mind is bypassed during hypnosis and acceptable suggestions are delivered [2]. It is a trance mental state that is later followed by giving suggestion. During hypnosis, suggestions are used to cure a lot of psychological health problems, such as stress, addiction, and phobia. It can as well assist in managing physical problems like pain reduction, such as the pain caused by chemotherapy in cancer patients [3].

In a trance, the normal state of the mind occurs regularly as when watching an engrossing movie, reading an absorbing book, or performing monotonous activity; thus hypnosis is also described as an "attentive, receptive focal concentration" [4]. It is commonly assumed that during hypnosis, the subconscious mind is in a suggestible state while the conscious mind is distracted or guided to become dormant [5].

Misperceptions about hypnosis by clinical practitioners and their clients have been shaped through years of inaccurate but interesting portrayals of hypnosis in books, plays, and movies. Part of the misperceptions is that individuals with seemingly magical powers to manipulate the unsuspecting innocent with their authoritative voice commands and penetrating eyes are depicted as hypnotists. For these reasons, witch doctors, evil scientists, space aliens, and vampires have all been portrayed as using hypnosis to achieve their dubious ends [6]. Hypnosis is introduced to others as a form of entertainment on television talk shows or at comedy clubs. Volunteers from the audience act out of fantasies to make the audience laugh from the hypnotist's simple commands for sleep and snaps of the fingers. The individuals hypnotized appear to apparently behave in ways that are contrary to normal behavior or out of character. However, some clinical practitioners themselves have contributed to further exacerbate this denigrative image of hypnosis [6]. This chapter will review the traditional and conventional approaches used in hypnosis, their advantages and disadvantages as well as where hypnosis is used as a complementary or alternative therapy to the modern day orthodox medicine.

1.1 Heart-rate variability as a measure of hypnotic depth

Ensuring sufficient depth to induce genuine hypnotic responsiveness is one of the major challenges in hypnotic research [7]. Hypnotic susceptibility, a stationary characteristic of a subject, is distinct from hypnotic depth, which is a dynamic property that represents the subject's momentary capacity for response to hypnotic suggestions [8].

Electro-encephalogram (EEG) is a candidate for monitoring neural activity. Higher power over the alpha, beta, and theta parietal region associated with sustained-attentional processing and greater EEG asymmetry was seen in the highly hypnotizable subjects [9].

In an investigation, heart rate, frequency of changes from a time-frequency analysis of heart-rate variability (HRV), and amplitude were compared with the continuous self-rated hypnotic depth (SRHD) of 10 volunteers. The investigation recorded significant linear relationships between the high-frequency (HF) component of the heart-rate variability (HRV) and the continuous self-rated hypnotic depth (SRHD), the continuous self-rated hypnotic depth (SRHD) correlated positively with the amplitude of the HF component and negatively with the frequency of the HF [10].

1.1.1 A brief insight into the similarities and differences between hypnosis and meditation

Generally, quieting of the mind is achieved during meditation, which may be compared with hypnosis. Meditation may qualify as hypnosis depending on the state achieved, especially if suggestions are given to achieve a desired effect. Although meditation may be self-directed, hypnosis can however occur naturally without formal induction [6].

1.1.2 Similarities between concentrative meditation and hypnosis

The concentration and attentional practices employed that result in an altered state are similar for both classical hypnosis and concentration meditation; the neurophysiology associated with those states and the phenomenology of those altered states are also similar [11].

Focusing attention by attempts to relax and concentrate the mind is the beginning of both meditation and hypnosis. The breath is the main focus of most meditators nowadays. Staring at a spot, watching pendulum swinging, etc., are ways of focusing and sustaining in hypnosis [7]. Hypnosis literature describes the method used to reach the state as suppressing competing thoughts, or as dis-attending to competing stimuli [12]. Ayya Khema described it in meditation literature as letting go of thoughts and perceptions [13].

Many types of meditation such as the Buddhist, Hindu, Christian, and Jewish emphasize on letting go of thoughts and concentration like the attentional focus procedures in hypnosis. In meditation, especially the Buddhist type, mindfulness practices are usually employed. Concentrative practice lets go of thoughts, focuses attention and shifts it to a subtler experience. Participants are trained in mindfulness meditation to describe mental states and activities in great detail and to observe the rapidly shifting thoughts, emotions, panorama of sensations, etc. [14, 15]. Concentration and mindfulness are both cultivated and work synergistically. Concentration is language associated ancient Buddhist that leads to altered states of consciousness and aims at serenity, one of which at least resembles deep sleep. Cognitive, emotional, and motivational changes as they increase in depth demonstrate an altered state called absorption [16]. Mindfulness aims at altered states of consciousness and provides an insight through observation of one's own mental processes. In behavioral medicine and pain management programs, Vipassana meditation has been used to teach patients how to become less reactive by objectifying their sensations [17]. Despite the fact that altered states are usually first identified by subjective experiences, relatively, the observation of one's own mental processes has been neglected in hypnosis research [11].

1.1.3 The altered states

Qualitative changes can be specified by absorption that is reached through concentration. The movement to absence of thought with prevailing calmness from the normal everyday mind with prevailing thoughts occurs in the four stages of absorption. The meditator's attention basically focuses first on an object and then on subtle experience increasingly, the phenomenal fields are then abandoned more and more. The movement of the meditator to a more peaceful happy feeling and then to composure from a stage of attendant physical experience with aroused positive emotion is achieved. In the fourth stage of absorption, a characteristic peaceful feeling of calmness is achieved with a very much aware mind like what one obtains in deep hypnosis [11].

Trained meditators usually can recognize these states of absorption and be able to report on the absence or presence of mental qualities such as feeling of joy or rupture, associative thinking, feeling of calmness, etc. Mindfulness is facilitated as the mind becomes quiet in concentrative meditation; however, mindfulness is not the principal goal of concentrative meditation. The meditator can report back on the qualities of the trance state observed [18].

There are at least two methods for assessing qualities of inner experience viz.: The Experience Analysis Technique [11, 19] and the Phenomenology of Consciousness Inventory or PCI [19, 20]; however, these methods have been underutilized [11].

1.1.4 Hypnosis and meditation phenomenology

Sustaining and focusing attention in both meditation and hypnosis lead to similar changes in mental state [21]. In a study involving two groups, Indian Kundalini meditators in one group and highly hypnotizables in the other. Directly, the two studies cannot be compared as they analyzed the data differently; however, both deep self-hypnosis and meditation were associated with alterations in self-awareness, state of awareness, perception, time sense and meaning with changes in imagery, rationality, and vividness due to elevation on Phenomenology of Consciousness Inventory (PCI), and both processes were accompanied with feelings of love and joy [11].

Comparing the PCI results for medium and deep absorptions (levels 1–2 vs. 3–4) described in Buddhist texts [22] with medium and deep levels of hypnosis [17] are other ways of similarities elaborations. Whether it is hypnosis or meditation, experience tends to be more vivid at medium levels and more aplomb at deep levels [11].

1.1.5 Differences between hypnosis and concentrative meditation

The difference between meditation and hypnosis has to do largely with expectancies and goals, and their relative emphasis on mindfulness (meditation) or suggestion (hypnosis) as well [11].

1.1.6 Practices and goals

Specific outcomes such as symptom removal are the basic interest for people seeking hypnosis, whereas, meditators' interest has to do with long-term goals having to do with insight, serenity, and enlightenment or spiritual liberation. Meditation is a solo experience, while hypnosis usually calls for two people except in self-hypnosis. Meditators spend years expectedly in developing their skill, it is however amazing to some patients if the hypnotist tells them that it will require more than one hypnosis session for their cure. Meditation involves daily practice for 20 minutes to an hour, then proceeding for a retreat where 10–15 hours of daily practice for several weeks or months is observed [11].

1.1.7 Expectancy

Meditators expect to see reality without bias through their "pure bright awareness" rather than suggestibility. People using hypnosis expect suggestibility, believing that the hypnotist will be able to change their perception and motivation profoundly by giving suggestion after entering an altered state; that is, they will not want a cigarette or feel pain [11].

1.2 The difference between hypnosis and hypnotherapy

Although hypnosis and hypnotherapy are words that are used rather interchangeably, the two words are not the same. Hypnosis is more a state of mind while hypnotherapy is the name of the therapeutic version in which hypnosis is used [23].

2. Traditional versus modern hypnosis

There are various types of hypnosis; however, the two distinct forms of hypnotherapy taught are the traditional, often referred to as, script-based approach, and the modern Ericksonian approach. They are sometimes better known as the direct or authoritative hypnosis and indirect or permissive hypnosis, respectively. The modern approaches are considered to be the conventional ways of inducing or achieving hypnosis.

In our society today, three main types of hypnosis are used to hypnotize another person or hypnotize one's self. These three types of hypnosis are traditional hypnosis, Ericksonian hypnosis, and self-hypnosis. Each type of hypnosis varies from one another in terms of practice and use. The three types of hypnosis have a common denominator; that is, they all begin with some form of hypnotic induction like fixed eye or counting backward to induce a hypnotic state [24].

2.1 Traditional hypnosis

Is the most widely used basic form of hypnosis due to the belief that anyone can do it with very little instruction and training. Traditional hypnosis is believed to be the easiest form of hypnosis, it relies on simple suggestions and commands. Traditional hypnosis uses direct commands and suggestions to influence a person's feelings, thoughts, behaviors, and actions once the subject is in a hypnotic state. Traditional hypnosis will only work on people who are easy to follow orders, the hypnotist will need to know whether the patient is critical or not before the hypnotic session begins [3]. Often, it is not considered entirely effective for people that have analytical and critical thought processes. Commands and suggestions are usually interfered by the conscious mind; the critique nature of the conscious mind does not allow messages to be fully absorbed by the subconscious [3]. Traditional hypnosis is also the basis for stage hypnotism, which is popular in today's culture among partygoers and comedy club attendees [3].

Despite being largely unchanged as a directive approach since the 1930s, traditional hypnosis is still the dominant approach taught in countries like Australia [3].

The hypnotist will ask you to close your eyes, relax and forget everything in your mind in a traditional hypnotic approach. Once you enter a trance mode, he will give you hypnotic suggestion. For instance, if the patient wants to stop smoking, in the therapy session the hypnotist might ask the subject to visualize the harms of smoking, how awful it smells and hurts the nose and eyes. The therapist will give the subject suggestions that when not smoking you will be alright. Any time the subject remembers to smoke, he will remember the awful smell from a cigarette. This will help the subject to stop smoking and this is how traditional hypnosis works [3]. According to some studies, the success rate of this form of hypnosis rarely exceeds 30%; although the client may feel better, there may be higher relapse rate and the client may not always do better the next time something similar happens [3].

In a situation when the traditional method does not work for the subject, the hypnotist might need to use another method like conversational hypnosis, etc. [3].

Unlike the traditional approach, conversational hypnosis is a type of hypnosis done to a subject or patient with the use of words and persuasion. It can also be used to treat stress, addiction, and phobia like in traditional hypnosis [3].

2.2 Modern hypnosis

The modern approach to hypnosis was developed by a renowned American psychiatrist and psychologist named Dr. Milton Erikson, thus named Eriksonian hypnosis. This method is built around understanding the client's unique situation and needs. The modern hypnosis approach will assist clients to build better cognitive skills and change the way they perceive a situation in and around challenging circumstances. Interventions are tailored toward the individuals' need, and this approach achieves a much higher success rate. Modern hypnosis particularly is an excellent approach for those who are skeptical of hypnosis as it uses metaphors rather than just direct suggestions [24]. Metaphors allow the brain to think creatively and arrive at conclusions that may not be reached by employing the more unilateral form of traditional hypnosis. Rather than simple commands and suggestions, metaphors work by comparing and contrasting two things in a more complex way [24]. The mind is allowed to wrap around an idea or thought in a more organic way than direct suggestion, skeptics are often able to be hypnotized using this approach than the traditional one. Modern Ericksonian hypnosis uses interspersal and isomorphic metaphors. Interspersal metaphors use embedded commands that distract the conscious mind, allowing the unconscious mind to process the message of the metaphors. Isomorphic metaphors tell a story that has a moral, which makes the unconscious mind draw a one-to-one comparison between the moral of the story and a problem or issue that it is already familiar with [24].

Neuro-linguistic programing (NLP) is a form of hypnosis used along with self-hypnosis to deal with issues such as self-esteem, self-confidence, and overall mental well-being. It is used also to conquer phobias and fears and to quell anxieties [24]. In NLP, the same thought process as a fear or problem is used to reverse or get rid of the problem; it is an effective method. Reframe, flash, and anchoring are the three different techniques used with NLP. NLP is most effective when the techniques are used all together or separately [24].

Self-hypnosis allows the mind when relaxed to reach a hypnotic state without a hypnotist or hypnotherapist. This form of hypnosis is performed by oneself to achieve a deep state of relaxation [8]. Suggestions and commands are made by oneself, or by an MP3 or a CD player that guides oneself in the hypnosis session. A lot of people who do not trust others with influential subconscious and fragile mind prefer self-hypnosis instead of the guided hypnosis [24].

2.3 Tools/techniques used in hypnosis induction

2.3.1 Hypnotic inductions

Hypnotic induction is the first process that a hypnotist uses to put the clients into a trance state where they are more open to suggestion. Some of the tools or techniques used in inducing hypnosis include the following:

2.3.2 Relaxation technique

One of the common techniques used by the therapist is relaxation, a relaxed client may fall into trance and his mind will be open to suggestion. Relaxed clients are more likely to talk to the therapist and be open to indirect suggestions. Some common methods of relaxation include: making the client comfortable, lying down, client's head counting down, controlled breathing, relaxing and tensing muscles, and speaking in soft tone [25].

2.3.3 Handshake technique

In most societies, handshakes are the commonest form of greetings, and Milton Erickson—the farther of hypnotherapy—famously used the handshake technique as a way to induce hypnotic trance. By the handshake, the subconscious mind is shocked by disrupting the common social norm. The hypnotist interrupts the pattern established by our mind by grabbing the wrist or pulling the subject forward and off balance, in an abnormal way of handshake. Suddenly, with the interrupted pattern, the subconscious mind is open for suggestions [25].

2.3.4 Arm levitation technique

Arm levitation technique is a classical Ericksonian technique of inducing hypnosis; this method begins with the clients closing their eyes and being asked to notice the difference between their arms. For instance, they might say the arm feels cold or hot, light or heavy. Suggestions are made by the hypnotist as to the sensations in each arm. In a trance mode, the clients may simply believe in their mind that they have lifted their arm or may physically lift their arm. In either way, successful induction is achieved [25].

2.3.5 Eyes cues

The right sphere of the brain manages creativity and consciousness while the left manages the practical and subconsciousness. During a conversation, the direction of the subject's eyes indicates the sphere accessed, looking right indicates accessing the consciousness and left the subconsciousness. If the eyes are accessing the subconscious, you can make a suggestion that they are not consciously aware (**Figure 1**). The eyes may as well be fixated on one object in the room. Stephen Brooks developed a new technique of inducing hypnosis on the listener with eye movements [25].

2.3.6 Visualization

Both trance and suggestions can be induced using the visualization technique. For instance, a subject can be asked to recall a room he is familiar with, to imaging every detail in the room such as the windows, the floor, the light, the wall, the painting etc. Afterward, the subject then moves into a room he is less familiar with. As the subject struggles to recall the exact details, his mind is open to suggestion. Visualization can be used to recall positive memories and positive images and experiences (wedding, birthday graduation) to change one's perception of a negative image [25].

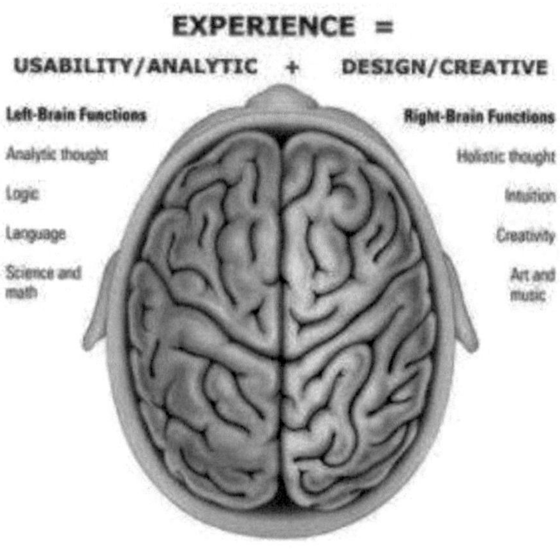

Figure 1.
Functions of the left and right brain spheres [25].

2.3.7 Falling backward/sudden shack

Shocked subjects can enter into a trance; a woman's foot was once stepped by Erickson, which was followed by suggestion. The sensation of falling backward, "trust fall," a milder version, shocks the system and opens the mind to suggestion; however, certainly the subject will not be dropped [25].

2.3.8 Eye fixation

Take for instance a situation when you find yourself "zoning out" and staring at an interesting item in the room while someone is talking. If you will completely miss what the person talking said, you may have been in a trance. One of the famous objects used in trance induction is "power pendulum" or a "swinging pocket watch" although any object can be used to achieve that. The object opens the subconscious mind to suggestion and keeps the conscious occupied [25].

2.3.9 Breathing countdown

In meditation, controlled breathing is used, it can as well act as an easy form of self-hypnosis.

The procedure is as follows:

- Close your eyes and sit upright in a chair, arms on your lap.
- Breathe deep through the nose and out through the mouth.
- Using slow controlled breaths, countdown from 100.
- Each exhale counts as one interval.
- At the end you may be in a trance. If not continue the exercise counting down from a higher number [25].

2.3.10 Body scan

Body scan is a popular method employed in self-hypnosis. Scanning begins from top of the body with your eyes closed, scan down slowly from the head to the feet. Every sensation should be noticed, your breath expanding the ribcage, chair on your back, the feet on the ground, each finger extended and the pain in your elbow. This process should be repeated from the bottom to the top, the scanning up and down should be continued until you enter trance. Other hypnotic induction techniques such as countdown breathing and relaxation can be stacked with body scan to increase effectiveness [25].

2.4 Hypnotic suggestions

The desired behavior to be performed by the client is referred to as suggestion. After a hypnotized person enters trance (a state in which the subject is more open to influence), post-hypnotic suggestions are delivered. Suggestions are classified into direct and indirect based on schools of thought [25].

2.4.1 Direct suggestion

An explicit command to perform certain action is known as a direct suggestion in conversational hypnosis. It is a powerful tool though viewed as unethical because of the authority or power a hypnotist has over the client. With this method, the client does not control the decision to change behavior. Some classical direct suggestions include:

- "You will stop smoking"
- "You will go to sleep"
- "You will lose weight" [25].

2.4.2 Indirect suggestion

Certified hypnotherapists use indirect suggestion as their favorite, Milton Erickson was a champion of indirect suggestion; in this method, the control is in the subject's hands rather than those of the authoritarian, the patient's boundaries and clinical ethics are respected. This method has proven to be more effective for subjects that are skeptical or resistant to trance. One could say: "When you are comfortable, you may wish to close your eyes" rather than "order" a subject to relax (direct suggestion) [25].

3. Advantages and disadvantages of traditional versus conventional approaches of achieving hypnosis and hypnotherapy

Traditional hypnosis is believed to be the simplest and easiest form of hypnotherapy that can be done even by oneself. As an advantage over conventional approach, traditional hypnosis is authoritative and can be a more powerful tool using direct suggestions [26]. As a disadvantage, this approach is commonly met with resistance [27]. The conventional or modern approach is a subtle, respectful method using indirect suggestions and has advantages of being accommodative, ethical, and more effective than the traditional method; the traditional approach is considered unethical by some schools of thought. Another disadvantage of the traditional approach is that some studies claim that this form of hypnosis rarely achieves more than a 30% success rate, and has a higher of rate relapse [3]. Although the clients may feel better, however, they may not always do better the next time something similar happens [3].

3.1 Hypnotic risks

Hypnosis has been shown to be associated with some risks according to the reviewed literature in the late 1980s. The literature documented a few cases of patients who displayed "unanticipated" adverse behavior after hypnosis [26]. Complications or adverse reactions usually encountered during hypnosis consisted of unexpected, unwanted thoughts, feelings, or behaviors during or after hypnosis that are inconsistent with agreed goals and interfere with the hypnotic process by impairing optimal mental function. Adverse reactions most commonly suspected included nausea, panic, dizziness, drowsiness, headache, stiffness, anxiety, and serious reactions such as masking of organic disorders and symptom substitution occasionally [26, 27]. Deficiencies in the hypnotist's techniques such as not knowing that suggestions in hypnosis are accepted literally, taking the patient rapidly out of trance, inappropriately using age regression, not prescreening for certain psychopathology, or preconceived expectations of negative consequences of hypnosis not being dispelled before initiating the session were considered to be the root cause of the problems [26].

4. The use of hypnosis/hypnotherapy as complementary or alternative approach to the modern day orthodox medicine

In the late 1700s when effective pharmaceutical and surgical treatment options were limited, hypnosis became a popular approach for the treatment of medical conditions [6]. As alternative treatments for medical conditions become popular, contemporary medicine is being challenged to take a more integrative approach. Hypnosis is used for conditions such as anxiety, depression, phobias, and attention deficit disorders not believed to be primarily psychological although the potential for a psychological basis exists for many of the mentioned conditions [6].

Hypnosis has been used effectively in a variety of medical settings such as chronic pain management, labor, surgery, dentistry, etc. Several studies reported its efficacy in the treatment of anxiety disorders [28–31].

For a variety of problems, hypnosis has been used as an adjunct to cognitive behavior therapy. Cognitive behavior therapy combined with hypnosis has been employed in the treatment of anxiety disorders, pain, depression, smoking cessation, obesity, and hypertension [6, 32].

The American Medical Association in 1958 and the American Psychological Association in 1960 approved the use of hypnosis as an adjunct treatment; in a variety of psychological and physical conditions, its efficacy has been established [33]. Mostly, contemporary applications of clinical hypnosis could be in four major areas viz.: behavioral, pshychological, medical, and self-development. The contemporary medical applications of hypnosis include medicine, surgery, and dentistry, the uses of which affect the somatic and behavioral aspects of the illness [34].

Although the traditional hypnotic approach is used for treating anxiety, depression, phobias, and attention deficit disorders, numerously, the modern or conventional approaches are employed in clinical hypnosis as either adjunct, complementary, or alternative therapy in present day orthodox medicine.

4.1 Behavioral and psychological applications of hypnosis

4.1.1 The potentials of hypnosis in the treatment of depressive disorders

Employment of more therapeutic techniques and procedures in the treatment of depression as in the treatment of any other psychological disorder make better chances of successful outcomes [35]. Hypnosis employed in many ways in a goal-directed fashion as a highly efficient and flexible tool makes it suitable to be incorporated into the treatment of depression. It may be used to reduce anxiety, increase responsiveness, interrupt negative ruminations, and establish positive expectancy [35]. In rigid and distorted patterns of thinking or interpreting events, hypnosis may be used more intensely to facilitate flexibility [35]. Alladin and Alibhai's [36] study of 2007 represents the first comparison of a treatment using hypnosis as an adjunct to a well-established psychological therapy for depression (Beck's Cognitive Behavioral Therapy for Depression) [36].

4.1.2 Treatment of anxiety disorders using hypnosis

The 1996 report by the National Institute of Health Technology Assessment Panel considered an effective and viable solution for the treatment of pain associated with cancer and many other chronic pain conditions [37]. Hypnotherapy has also been reported effective for anxiolysis in acute pain, analgesia, and emesis [38]. Brugnoli et al. [39] also reported the effectives of hypnosis for anxiety management as an adjunct therapy for patients receiving palliative care in chronic diseases conditions.

4.1.3 Cessation of smoking

Hypnosis has been used as an adjunct cognitive behavior therapy for smoking cessation. Combined hypnotic and cognitive behavior therapy treatment for smoking cessation was found to be superior to a wait-list control condition as [40]. In 1988, these results were replicated in a study comparing larger sample sizes with the same conditions [41].

4.1.4 Use of hypnosis in mental health nursing

The Ericksonian hypnosis supports nursing goals of honoring and respecting patient individuality, and, therefore, has been advocated for use in mental health nursing by Zahourek [42].

4.2 Medical applications of hypnosis

4.2.1 Management of allergy

As suggested by some early literature, many allergies have an emotional basis, thus could be treated using a hypnotic approach [43]. However, studies have shown that hypnosis may alter body's physiological response to various stimuli [44]. The positive effects of social support on natural killer cell activity and cortisol levels have been shown by some researchers, this has implications for cancer progression [45].

4.2.2 Treatment of impotence

A strong potential of hypnosis for managing impotence has been documented in the medical literature since 1960s [39], and this claim has been supported by recent clinical trials, 88% success rate was reported using hypnosis for impotence in almost 3000 patients [46]. Using hypnosis and acupuncture, 75% success rate was recorded in treating impotence [47].

4.2.3 Emesis

Many a times, chemotherapy is associated with adverse effects of nausea and vomiting, these unwanted side effects among others are reduced by hypnotherapy. The need for antiemetic drugs was reduced significantly by using hypnosis to manage chemotherapeutic adverse effects in children with anticipatory nausea and vomiting [48].

4.2.4 Management of gastrointestinal disorders

One of the commonest disorders found in the practice of gastroenterology is irritable bowel syndrome (IBS), the etiology of which is complex, emotional stress, anger, and depression negatively affect IBS, thereby worsening the symptoms of the disorder. The intervention that has empirically demonstrated to be more efficacious in treating IBS is the use of hypnosis as an adjunct to cognitive behavior therapy. An important impact of hypnotic treatment lasting for several years in most patients has been shown in most patients suffering from irritable bowel syndrome [32].

4.2.5 Obstetrics

Experience of patients treated with hypnosis at birth was satisfactory [49], hypnosis has also been used to facilitate delivery in obstetrics [50], and shorter labor [51], and requires the use of significantly less analgesic medications [32].

4.2.6 Pulmonary medicine

Hypnosis has been shown to improve pulmonary functioning in asthmatic patients with high and medium hypnotizability [52, 53]. Brown [54] reported the efficacy of hypnosis for managing emotional states exacerbating airways obstruction.

4.2.7 Application of hypnosis in clinical pain management

Demonstratively, analogue pain has been reduced by hypnosis, preliminary information concerning possible physiological mechanisms of hypnotic analgesia has been offered by studies showing central nervous system activity during hypnotic procedures [55]. In another study, the effectiveness of hypnosis on pain reduction has been demonstrated, which contributed to the theoretical understanding of hypnotic analgesia [55]. These findings were taken to a new level of sophistication by some neurophysiological studies [56]. As an adjunct therapy, clinical hypnosis was considered effective for pain reduction in cancer patients as well as severe chronic diseases for patients receiving palliative care [38]. In the management of chronic pain or cancer procedure-related pain in children, hypnosis is considered as an effective technique [56]. Pain reduction was reported in patients having metastatic breast carcinoma by hypnotic approach [57].

4.2.8 Efficacy of hypnosis in the treatment of headache and migraine

Hypnosis fulfills the research criteria in clinical psychology for it to be considered a well-established efficacious treatment for headache and migraine [58, 59]. No risks of adverse reactions or side effects are produced by hypnosis; this decreases the cost of medication associated to conventional medical treatments [59].

4.2.9 Use of hypnosis and acupuncture for pain relief

There exists an inherent relationship between acupuncture as a form of traditional Chinese medicine and hypnotic rituals of awareness under conscious hypnosis. Besides its various competent applications in different fields, it is used in surgical operations as the sole anesthetic for pain relief, and also for patient care during pre-, post-, and intra-operative periods [60].

4.2.10 Hypnoanalgesia

Benefits of pain relief by hypnosis have been documented in numerous studies. Pin prick and laser heat pain stimulation studies, followed by direct suggestions in hypnosis, resulted in decreased pain measured by means of pain-related brain potentials both subjectively and objectively [61]. Hypnoanalgesia was reported for repair of atrial septal defects in three patients and for mitral commissurotomy in four patients, using hypnosis as the sole method of anesthesia for one of the patients [62].

4.2.11 Identification of human sexuality

In practice, therapists are often confronted with patients seeking therapy for challenges they face owing to their deep-rooted economic, ethical, family, political, religious, and social backgrounds. Therapists find old and newer hypnotic techniques handy in managing the patients' gender ambivalence, identity, sexual orientation, preferences, and functioning difficulties [63–66].

4.3 Application of hypnosis in performance enhancement

4.3.1 Performance enhancement

Sport hypnosis helps enhance performance and well-being of an athlete or a user. This form of hypnosis is based on three combined techniques of mental training procedures: self-hypnosis, eyes-open hypnosis, and traditional eye-closed hypnosis. It is a form of alert hypnosis. Post-hypnotic signals or triggers and rhythmic athletic activities can induce sport hypnotic state (SHS) [63]. An alternative state of consciousness is achieved; performance in sport hypnotic state happens in a flow sate, which increases results despite decreased effort, known otherwise as "relaxed effectiveness." Olympic Games champions' reports show that peak performance is achieved through sport hypnotic state training. In the quest for excellent performance, sport hypnosis techniques can also be applied [67].

5. Conclusion

Despite the pejorative image display of hypnosis and misconceptions surrounding it, hypnosis still has numerous applications in contemporary medicine. Hypnotherapy conducted by a trained therapist is considered as a complementary or safe alternative to present day orthodox medication for numerous ailments.

Author details

Mikail Hudu Garba[1*] and Mohammed Mamman[2]

1 Department of Pharmacology and Toxicology, Faculty of Veterinary Medicine, University of Abuja, Nigeria

2 Department of Pharmacology and Toxicology, Faculty of Veterinary Medicine, Ahmadu Bello University, Zaria, Nigeria

*Address all correspondence to: mghudu@yahoo.com

References

[1] Geers M. Hypnotherapy- volume I COURSE 100. International medical and dental hypnotherapy association (IMDHA) and International Association of Counselors and Therapists (IACT). 2016. Available from: www.hypnosisalliance.com

[2] Fromm E. Significant developments in clinical hypnosis during the past 25 years. The International Journal of Clinical and Experimental Hypnosis. 1987;**35**:215-230

[3] Sani I. What Is Traditional Hypnosis? 2011. Available from: https://EzineArticles.com/expert/Ian_Sani/130890

[4] Spiegel H, Greenleaf M, Spiegel D. Hypnosis. In: Sadock BJ, Sadock VA, editors. Kaplan & Sadock's Comprehensive Textbook of Psychiatry. 7th ed. Vol. 2. Philadelphia, Pa: Lippincott Williams & Wilkins; 2000. p. 21382146

[5] Stewart JH. Hypnosis in contemporary medicine. Mayo Clinic Proceedings. 2005;**80**(4):511-524

[6] Chapman RA. Introduction to cognitive behavior therapy and hyonosis. In: Chapman RA, editor. The Clinical Use of Hypnosis in Cognitive Behavior Therapy: A Practitioner's Casebook. New York, NY: Springer Publishing Company; 2006. p. 3

[7] Barabasz A, Christensen C. Age regression: Tailored versus scripted inductions. American Journal of Clinical Hypnosis. 2006;**48**:251-261

[8] Shor RE, Orne EC. Norms on the Harvard group scale of hypnotic susceptibility, form A. The International Journal of Clinical and Experimental Hypnosis. 1963;**11**:39-47

[9] Crawford HJ, Clarke SW, Kitner-Triolo M. Self-generated happy and sad emotions in low and highly hypnotizable persons during waking and hypnosis: Laterality and regional EEG activity differences. International Journal of Psychophysiology. 1996;**24**:239-266

[10] Diamond SG, Davis OC, Howe RD. Heart-rate variability as a quantitative measure of hypnotic depth. Intl. Journal of Clinical and Experimental Hypnosis. 2008;**56**(1):1-18. DOI: 10.1080/00207140701672961

[11] Holroyd J. The science of meditation and the state of hypnosis. American Journal of Clinical Hypnosis. 2003;**46**:2. Available from: www.asch.net/portals/0/journallibrary/articles/ajch-46/holroyd.pdf

[12] Crawford HJ. Brain dynamics and hypnosis: Attentional and disattentional processes. International Journal of Clinical and Experimental Hypnosis. 1994;**42**:204-232. DOI: 10.1080/00207149408409352

[13] Khema A. Who is Myself? A guide to Buddhist Meditation. Boston: Wisdom publications; 1997. [based on Sutta 9, the states of consciousness Sutta, in M. Walshe, trans. (1987). The long discourses of the Buddha. Boston: Wisdom.]. Available from: https://www.amazon.com/Who-My-Self-Buddhist-Meditation/dp/0861711270

[14] Shear J, Jevning R. Pure consciousness: Scientific exploration of meditation techniques. Journal of Consciousness Studies. 1999;**6**(2-3): 189-209. Available from: https://psycnet.apa.org/record/1999-10821-009

[15] Wallace BA. The Buddhist tradition of samatha: Methods for refining and examining consciousness. Journal of Consciousness Studies. 1999;**6**:175-187.

Available from: https://philpapers.org/rec/WALTBT

[16] Bucknell RS. Reinterpreting the jhanas. Journal of the International Association of Buddhist Studies. 1993;**16**(2):375-409. Available from: https://journals.ub.uni-heidelberg.de/index.php/jiabs/article/.../8818/2725

[17] Kabat-Zinn J. An outpatient program in behavioral medicine for chronic pain patients based on the practice of mindfulness meditation: Theoretical considerations and preliminary results. General Hospital Psychiatry. 1982;**4**:33-47. DOI: 10.1016/0163-8343(82)90026-3

[18] Brown DP. A model for the levels of concentrative meditation. International Journal of Clinical and Experimental Hypnosis. 1977;**25**(4):236-273. DOI: 10.1080/00207147708415984

[19] Pekala RJ, Kuma VK, Ronald Maurer MA. The Phenomenology of Consciousness Inventory Hypnotic Assessment Procedure (PCI-HAP): Administrator's Manual. [PCI-HAP. Administrator's Manual. 100509.doc]. 2009. pp. 1-28

[20] Cardena EA. The phenomenology of quiescent and physically active deep hypnosis. The International Journal of Clinical and Experimental Hypnosis. 2005;**53**(1):37-59. DOI: 10.1080/00207140490914234

[21] Pekala RJ, Kumar VK. Operationalizing "trance" I: Rationale and research using a psychophenomenological approach. American Journal of Clinical Hypnosis. 2000;**43**:107-135. DOI: 10.1080/00029157.2000.10404265

[22] Thanissaro B. Samadhanga Sutta: The factors of concentration (AN 5.28), translated from the Pali by Thanissaro Bhikkhu. Access on insight (BCBS edition). 2013. Available from: https://www.accesstoinsight.org/tipitaka/an/an05/an05.028.than.html

[23] Zimberoff D. What Is the Difference Between Hypnosis and Hypnotherapy? How does hypnotherapy work? The wellness institute blog. Posted on Mar 22, 2018 11:15:00 AM; 2018

[24] Moore J. Types of Hypnosis. 2011. Available from: https://www.selfdevelopment.net/hypnosis/hypnosishypnotism/types-of-hypnosis

[25] Brooks S. Hypnotic Techniques A Comprehensive Guide. 2019. Available from: https://britishhypnosisresearch.com/hypnosis-techniques

[26] MacHovec F. Hypnosis complications, risk factors, and prevention. The American Journal of Clinical Hypnosis. 1988;**31**:40-49

[27] Lynn SJ, Martin DJ, Frauman DC. Does hypnosis pose special risks for negative effects? A master class commentary. The International Journal of Clinical and Experimental Hypnosis. 1996;**44**:719

[28] Alladin A. Handbook of Cognitive Hypnotherapy for Depression: An Evidence-Based Approach. Philadelphia: Wolters Kluwer Health/Lippincott Williams & Wilkins; 2007

[29] Brann L, Owens J, Williamson A. The Handbook of Contemporary Clinical Hypnosis: Theory and Practice. Chichester, West Sussex, UK: John Wiley & Sons; 2011

[30] Lynn SJ, Kirsch.I, and Rhue J.W. An introduction to clinical hypnosis. In: Lynn SJ, Rhue JW, Kirsch I, editors. Handbook of Clinical Hypnosis. 2nd ed. Washington, DC, US: American Psychological Association; 2010. pp. 3-18

[31] Nash MR, Barnier AJ. The Oxford Handbook of Hypnosis: Theory,

Research, and Practice. New-York, NY, US: Oxford University Press; 2008

[32] Mendoza ME, Capafons A. Efficacy of clinical hypnosis: A summary of its empirical evidence. Papeles del Psicólogo. 2009;**30**(2):98-116

[33] Mottern R. Using hypnosis as adjunct care in mental health nursing. Journal of Psychosocial Nursing. 2010;**48**(10):41-44

[34] Ginandes C. The strategic induction of hypnosis and CBT for the treatment of mind/body conditions. In: Chapman AT, editor. The Clinical Use of Hypnosis in Cognitive Behavior Therapy: A Practitioner's Casebook. New York, NY: Springer Publishing Company; 2006. pp. 243-245

[35] Al Rubaie T. The hypnotic treatment of depression. Alternative Health Practitioner. Fall. 1999;**5**(2):151-162

[36] Alladin A, Alibhai A. Cognitive hypnotherapy for depression: An empirical investigation. International Journal of Clinical and Experimental Hypnosis. 2007;**55**:147-166

[37] Lynn SJ, Kirsch I, Barabasz A, Cardena E, Patterson D. Hypnosis as an empirically supported clinical intervention: The state of the evidence and a look to the future. The International Journal of Clinical and Experimental Hypnosis. 2000;**48**(2):239-259

[38] Néron S, Stephenson R. Effectiveness of hypnotherapy with Cancer Patients' trajectory: Emesis, acute pain, and analgesia and Anxiolysis in procedures. The International Journal of Clinical and Experimental Hypnosis. 2007;**55**(3):336-354

[39] Brugnoli MP, Pesce G, Pasin E, Basile MF, Tamburin S, Polati E. The role of clinical hypnosis and self-hypnosis to relief pain and anxiety in severe chronic diseases in palliative care: A 2-year longterm follow-up of treatment in a nonrandomized clinical trial. Annals of Palliative Medicine. 2018;**7**(1):17-31

[40] Jeffrey TB, Jeffrey LK, Greuling JW, Gentry WR. Evaluation of a brief group treatment package including hypnotic induction for maintenance of smoking cessation: A brief communication. International Journal of Clinical and Experimental Hypnosis. 1985;**33**:95-98

[41] Jeffrey TB, Jeffrey LK. Exclusion therapy in smoking cessation: A brief communication. International Journal of Clinical and Experimental Hypnosis. 1988;**36**:70-74

[42] Zahourek RP. Utilizing Ericksonian hypnosis in psychiatric-mental health nursing. Perspectives in Psychiatric Care. 2002;**38**:15-22

[43] Elman D. Hypnotherapy. Glendale, Calif: Westwood Publishing Company; 1964

[44] Black S. Inhibition of immediate-type hypersensitivity response by direct suggestion under hypnosis. British Medical Journal. 1963;**1**:925-929

[45] Spiegel D, Sephton SE. Psycho-neuroimmune and endocrine pathways in cancer: Effects of stress and support. Seminars in Clinical Neuropsychiatry. 2001;**6**:252-265

[46] Crasilneck HB. Hypnotic techniques for smoking control and psychogenic impotence. The American Journal of Clinical Hypnosis. 1990;**32**:147-153

[47] Aydin S, Ercan M, Caskurlu T, et al. Acupuncture and hypnotic suggestions in the treatment of non-organic male sexual dysfunction. Scandinavian Journal of Urology and Nephrology. 1997;**31**:271-274

[48] Zeltzer LK, Dolgin MJ, LeBaron S, LeBaron C. A randomized, controlled study of behavioral intervention for chemotherapy distress in children with cancer. Pediatrics. 1991;**88**:34-42

[49] Pinnell CM, Covino NA. Empirical findings on the use of hypnosis in medicine: A critical review. International Journal of Clinical and Experimental Hypnosis. 2000;**48**:170-194

[50] Freeman RM, MacCauley AJ, Ev L, Chamberlain GVP. Randomized trial of self-hypnosis for analgesia in labour. British Medical Journal. 1986;**292**:657-658

[51] Jenkins MW, Pritchard MH. Hypnosis: Practical applications and theoretical considerations in normal labour. British Journal of Obstetrics and Gynaecology. 1993;**100**:221-226

[52] Ewer TC, Stewart DE. Improvement in bronchial hyper-responsiveness in patients with moderate asthma after treatment with a hypnotic technique: A randomized controlled trial. British Medical Journal. 1986;**293**:1129-1132

[53] Ben-Zvi Z, Spohn WA, Young SH, Kattan M. Hypnosis for exercise-induced asthma. The American Review of Respiratory Disease. 1982;**125**:392395

[54] Brown D. Evidence-based hypnotherapy for asthma: A critical review. International Journal of Clinical and Experimental Hypnosis. 2007;**55**:22-249

[55] Patterson DR, Jense MP. Hypnosis and clinical pain. Psychological Bulletin. 2003;**129**(4):495-521

[56] Tomé-Pires C, Miró J. Hypnosis for the management of chronic and cancer procedure-related pain in children. International Journal of Clinical and Experimental Hypnosis. 2012;**60**(4):432-457

[57] Spiegel D, Bloom JR. Group therapy and hypnosis reduce metastatic breast carcinoma pain. Psychosomatic Medicine. 1983;**45**:333339

[58] Hammond DC. Review of the efficacy of clinical hypnosis with headaches and migraines. International Journal of Clinical and Experimental Hypnosis. 2007;**55**:207-219

[59] Melis PM, Rooimans W, Spierings EL, Hoogduin CA. Treatment of chronic tension-type headache with hypnotherapy: A single-blind time controlled study. Headache. 1991;**31**:686-689

[60] Öztürk AÖ, Öztürk G. The inherent relationship between Traditional Chinese Medicine (TCM) and Hypnotic Rituals of Awareness Under Conscious Hypnosis (AUCH©) method. Journal of Complementary Medicine and Alternative Healthcare. 2018;**5**(2):JCMAH.MS.ID.555660

[61] Zachariae R, Bjerring P. The effect of hypnotically induced analgesia on flare reaction of the cutaneous histamine prick test. Archives of Dermatological Research. 1990;**282**:539-543

[62] Marmer MJ. Hypnoanalgesia and hypnoanesthesia for cardiac surgery. Journal of the American Medical Association. 1959;**171**:512-517

[63] Barkley R, Mosher E. Sexuality and hispanic culture: Counseling with children and their parents. Journal of Sex Education Therapy. 1995;**21**:255-267

[64] Williams E, Ellison F. Culturally informed social work practice with American Indian clients: Guidelines for non-Indian social workers. Journal of the National Association of Social Workers. 1996;**41**:147-151

[65] Zamora-Hernandez C, Patterson D. Homosexually active Latino

men: Issues for social work practice. In: Longres J, editor. Men of Color. New York: Harrington Park Press; 1996

[66] Daniel A. Hypnosis in human sexuality problems. American Journal of Clinical Hypnosis. 2005;**47**(4):229-242

[67] Unestahl LE. Alert, eyes-open sport hypnosis. American Journal of Clinical Hypnosis. 2018;**61**:159-172. DOI: 10.1080/00029157.2018.1491387

Section 2

New Scientific Approaches to Hypnosis

Chapter 3

The Integrative Theory of Hypnosis in the Light of Clinical Hypnotherapy

Rashit Tukaev

Abstract

The chapter describes the author's integrative theory of hypnosis and hypnotherapy (ITHH) and the universal hypnotherapy (UH) method. The ITHH contains neurophysiological, biological, and communicative components. (1) Hypnosis is triggered by symbolical hypnogenic situations of inability of decision-making and/or its behavioral realization. Hypnosis development results in qualitative reorganization of the brain activation system functioning from distribution to generation of activity. Hypnosis deepening is based on the increase of brain activation. Hypnosis development in right-handers is associated with a regressive reorganization of the left hemisphere to the right hemisphere functioning mode, with whole brain functioning on right hemispheric principle. (2) Hypnotization generates hypnogenic stress. Hypnotherapy activates a readaptation process, including neurohormonal, neurotransmitter secretions; activation of the immunological and biochemical responses; and spontaneous change of pain sensation. (3) Hypnotic communication styles (directive, non-directive) are (i) changing due to historical evolution of social communication styles and (ii) indirectly using the representations about hypnosis. The UH utilizes the ITHH, being close to the positive and mindfulness psychotherapeutic approaches. The complex of UH and psycho-education formed positive-dialogue psychotherapy (PDP) for the treatment of anxiety disorders. The randomized clinical trial of PDP efficiency in the therapy of panic and generalized anxiety disorders confirmed high clinical efficiency and the mindfulness effect of UH.

Keywords: hypnosis, theory, secondary-phenomenological approach, neurophysiology, hypnogenic situation, brain activation system, biology, communication, universal hypnotherapy, positive-dialogue psychotherapy, panic disorder, generalized anxiety disorder, randomized clinical trial, efficiency of psychotherapy, mindfulness effect

1. Introduction

The author's long-term work in the fields of hypnology and hypnotherapy revealed restrictions associated with the lacks of consistency and interdisciplinarity of the research and practice.

The phenomenon of animal hypnosis, identified in all higher vertebrates and, therefore, genetically determined [1, 2], as a rule, is not evaluated by modern hypnologists as a homolog of human hypnosis. The belonging of humans to mammals gives no chance for selective "loss" of basic, genetically determined protective mechanisms of hypnosis. If the ability of hypnotization in humans is genetically determined, how one can be fundamentally non-hypnable? In this logic, situational hypnability/non-hypnability is the result of the interaction of cultural and personal representations about hypnosis with the perception of actual hypnotization, personal request for hypnotization, but not the implementation of some primary, essential level of hypnability. What is the point of populational and longitudinal studies of hypnability and creation of great amount of appropriate psychometric tools for its estimation? What is measured in reality, hypnability or suggestibility? Where is the analysis of the results of clinical practice in which the vast majority of hypnotherapist's patients are hypnable?

It should be noted that the general trend for searching of interrelations between genetic factors and brain activities, especially in cases of mental disorders [3, 4], is accepted by modern hypnology [5, 6]. In the logic of the cognitive hypnosis paradigm, the relationship of the dopamine-related catechol-O-methyltransferase (COMT) [5] and the serotonin-related 5-HTTLPR polymorphisms to measuring hypnotizability was studied [6]. The study of connections between genotype and the hypnotizability, determined both by questionnaires, outside hypnosis, and in combination with real hypnosis [7] concretizes interrelations of dopaminergic and serotonergic genotypes and the subjective different experiences in hypnosis. From the standpoint of clinical hypnotherapy, which demonstrates efficiency in the treatment of anxiety and affective disorders [8], the fact of cross-association of the Val158Met catechol-O-methyltransferase genetic polymorphism simultaneously with (1) anxiety disorders (ADs) [9] and (2) hypnotizability [6] becomes significant.

The long-term process of accumulation of genetic data associated with the phenomenon of human hypnosis in the future can lead to a comparison of human and animal hypnosis. The search for the genetic basis of universal protective hypnosis reaction in humans and animals has not yet been realized.

The brain of all higher vertebrates operates in the fundamental circadian cycle of the steady states (modes) of sleep and wakefulness. The phenomenon of animal hypnosis represents a protective adaptation to the behavioral situations of an insoluble impasse [10, 11], which includes a holistic systemic pattern associated with immobilization (catalepsy); decrease or cessation of pain sensitivity; and situationally determined duration. Sleep and wakefulness form a category of circadian-conditioned, fundamental, stable states, whereas the phenomenon of hypnosis belongs a qualitatively different category of behaviorally situationally developing state that ends when the situation is resolved successfully. Such a logic allows us to distinguish between two basic genetically determined categories or classes of states in the activity of the brain: (1) circadian-conditioned sleep and wakefulness and (2) situationally determined (animal) hypnosis.

Russian neurophysiologists Bogdanov and Galashina [1, 2, 12] in the study of animal hypnosis in rabbits had revealed that the single case of animal hypnosis has long-term (1 month) neurobiological action; is followed by functional regress of neuronal activity in the networks, with reorganizational transduction of pathways of coded information, and restoration of neuronal activity after hypnosis; and stimulates and optimizes the learning in a previously actualized area of the behavior. So, experimental data indicate a powerful neurobiological effect of animal hypnosis, and increasing the effectiveness of learning in a previously actualized area acquires a fundamental therapeutic value in human hypnosis [12].

Being a homolog of animal hypnosis, human hypnosis extensively and variably implements a genetically defined neurophysiological pattern of adaptive response to behavioral impasse, complementing the range of triggers by symbolic impasses, due to thinking, culture. Moreover, traditional culture, and then therapy, channeling the use of the given neurophysiological pattern-state in various ways creates different types of its utilization and nominalization, defining it as hypnosis, trance, meditation, relaxation, etc.

The extreme adaptive and regressive nature of animal hypnosis (to overcome the behavioral impasse) determines the presence in this phenomenon of explicit systemic neurobiological and general biological adaptive mechanisms, which are inevitably realized in human hypnosis. Thus, the acceptance of conclusion about the fundamental unity of animal and human hypnosis not only stimulates the theoretical analysis of this phenomenon and development of related therapeutic practices but also targets the areas of research and outlines potential results.

2. The integrative theory of hypnosis

2.1 History of development and components

In the 1970s to 1980s, the author conducted an extensive research on the characteristics of reproduction and the impact of hypnosis-induced colors and images in the interest of their utilization in hypnotherapy of anxiety disorders [10, 11].

In the 1970s, Russian hypnology was based on Pavlov's theory of hypnosis, and the phenomenology of hypnosis was completely studied [10]. In an attempt to use color suggestion for additional directed (sedative, activating, based on the psychology of color) effects, the author began to use regular suggestion of blue color for the therapy of anxiety disorders. Like the Western colleagues, the author believed in the direct implementation of the "correct" hypnotic suggestion and expected that in deep hypnosis, patients would directly realize the suggestion of concrete blue color. Results of the suggestion, "To see the blue color, to see it constantly," turned out to be much more complicated (see **Figures 1–4**): (1) "vision" of color occurred not only in deep but also in medium hypnosis, i.e., in most patients; and (2) in addition to blue, other chromatic and achromatic colors and visual images were realized. Since the identified phenomenology of realization of color suggestion was not previously known, the author began its independent study, which lasted 10 years. Four voluminous studies were conducted:

1. The study of patterns of reproduction of hypnotically inducted colors and images, depending on the hypnosis depth (healthy subjects, 62; neurotic patients, 131)

2. The study of the phenomenon of chromatic and achromatic transformations of the blue color (healthy teenagers, 44; healthy adults, 63; neurotic patients, 158; patients with organic disorders, 156)

3. The study of spontaneous structures in the reproduction of hypnotically inducted colors (105 patients)

4. The study of the psychophysiological effects of hypnotically inducted color sensations and images (totally 85 healthy individuals, 90 patients)

For each study, special questionnaires were developed. Results obtained in the 1970s and 1980s were published in two author's monographs, given in the reference; therefore, this chapter contains only the main, valid results.

The experience obtained in the study of the hypnotic reproduction of color sensations and images is probably unique in its focus on the identification, fixation,

Figure 1.
The post-hypnotic drawings of hypnotized subjects, reflecting the reproduction of induced blue color: "To see, to represent, to feel the blue color." Illustrations from the author's monograph.

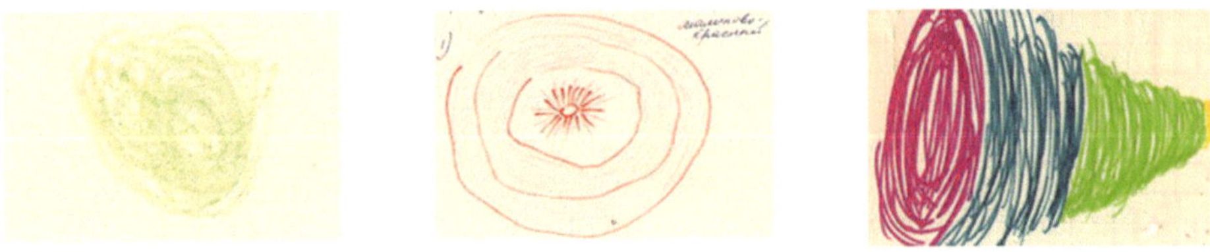

Figure 2.
The phenomenon of the chromatic transformation of hypnotically induced color. Posthypnotic drawings of subjects.

and detailed analysis of the spontaneous variability of the hypnotized response to suggestions in hypnosis. The study is focused not on assessing the effective achievement of a particular suggested result but on spontaneous responses to

Figure 3.
The phenomenon of the achromatic transformation of induced blue color. Posthypnotic drawings of subjects.

Figure 4.
Patterns of reproduction of color and image in dependence of hypnosis depth. Posthypnotic drawings of subjects. Note: picture's systematization was based on independent estimation of hypnosis depth during hypnosis session.

"banal" suggestion or spontaneous trance characteristics during hypnotherapy. Therefore, the phenomena described by the author fall out of sight of modern researchers of color suggestions in hypnosis [13, 14].

As a result of our research, a new systematization of the reproduction of suggested colors was obtained. It included (1) patterns of reproduction of the induced color and image in different depths of hypnosis; (2) the description and interpretation of a phenomenon of chromatic transformation of the induced color; and (3) the description and interpretation of a phenomenon of achromatic transformation of the induced color.

We described the spatial and temporal differences in the reproduction of color and image in medium and deep hypnosis. In medium hypnosis induced colors and images are reproduced two-dimensionally (flat) and wavelike damped. In deep hypnosis induced colors and images are reproduced three-dimensionally and stable over time. The hypnosis maximum depth is characterized by "effect of presence," when hypnotized find himself "in the reality of image"—the image becomes sensory multimodal.

The phenomenon of chromatic transformation of the induced color manifested in the reproduction of another color instead induced (e.g., red, yellow, green—on induction of blue). The study pointed to the connection of this phenomenon with infantilism—as personality characteristics of a hypnotized subject: (1) age-related (adolescents) and (2) disorder-related (dissociative disorders).

The phenomenon of achromatic transformation of the induced color manifests in decolorization of induced colors (into black, gray). According to our findings, the phenomenon of achromatic transformation of reproduced colors in hypnosis intensely increased in cases of brain organic disorders, which lead to the idea of its connection with low level of brain activation. The experimental verification confirmed the hypothesis. We received a change in the initial reproduction of blue color by psychopharmacological increase (imipramine) and decrease (chlorpromazine) of the level of activity of the reticular formation of the brain. A single use of imipramine (25 mg 1 h before a hypnotic session) validly improved color reproduction, and a single use of chlorpromazine (25 mg 1 h before a hypnotic session) caused a total achromatic transformation in all subjects.

The obtained results allowed us in the 1980s to 1990s to develop the secondary-phenomenological approach of the study of hypnosis [10, 11]. It is based on the following: (1) Identification of patterns of reproduction of induced colors and images depending on the hypnosis depth, age, healthy subjects, and anxiety and organic disorders. (2) Comparison of hypnotic visual phenomenological patterns with neurophysiological models of brain activation system, visual afterimages, age dynamics of hemispheric asymmetry, and construction of the neurophysiological model of hypnosis. (3) Comparison of modern data of hypnosis neurophysiology.

The secondary-phenomenological approach allowed us to move from the systemic phenomenological description of visual hypnosis to its neurophysiological modeling.

The secondary-phenomenological approach to the study of hypnosis is fundamentally close and presents the precursor of the methodology of studying neuronal correlates of consciousness developed in modern psychology of consciousness [15], in which the implementation of consciousness patterns is related to the neurophysiological activity of the brain that provides them.

In the 1980s to 1990s, we have investigated the biological mechanisms of hypnotherapy and hypnosis phenomenon of spontaneous nociception [10, 11]. The study of the biological mechanisms of hypnotherapy was based on results of systemic clinical research of blood system in dynamics of hypnotherapy of anxiety and organic disorders.

The study was based on a fourfold analysis of 29 blood components (clinical, biochemical, immunological): (1) at the beginning of therapy, before and after a hypnotherapy session and (2) at the end of therapy, before and after a hypnotherapy session. The groups of the study include 113 patients with anxiety disorders of neurotic (78 subjects) and organic (35 subjects) genesis. The description of the biological mechanisms of hypnotherapy was based on the valid data of statistical analyzes (parametric, nonparametric, factorial).

The last 30 years, we have conducted research on therapy and hypnotherapy communication mechanisms. These studies formed the basis for the description of the communicative component of hypnotherapy [14].

Studies have allowed us to develop the integrative theory of hypnosis, represented by neurophysiological, biological, and communicative components [10, 11, 16].

2.2 Neurophysiological component

The development of hypnosis is achieved through the creation of primary (for man and animal) or secondary (symbolical) hypnogenic situations which restricts the ability to make decisions and/or its behavioral expressions. Hypnosis development results in a qualitative reorganization of the brain activation system functioning from distribution to generation of activity. The functions of distribution and generation of activity are realized by morphologically different structures within the activating system of the brain.

Deepening of hypnosis from wakefulness to somnambulism is based on the growth of opportunities for brain activation; deep hypnosis opportunities for brain activation are comparable to the waking state.

Hypnosis development in right-handers is associated with a regressive transfer of the left hemisphere regulatory activity to the right hemispheric functioning mode. In comparison with the ontogenetic shift of hemispheric specialization, this is a reversed process of the whole brain function reorganization to right hemispheric principle. This conclusion was published in 1996 [10]. A year later, in 1997, the authoritative American hypnotist published a review with the characteristic title [17]: “Relateralizing hypnosis: or, have we been barking up the wrong hemisphere?”

Subsequent functional magnetic resonance imaging (fMRI) research showed [18, 19] high levels of activity in areas responsible for visualizing scenes (the occipital lobes) and for analyzing verbally presented scenarios (the left temporal lobe), a heightened activity in the prefrontal cortex, and a higher connectivity between different brain regions in highly hypnotizable people. In hypnosis, a perception of color, real or hallucinated, led to the activation of the fusiform area with more clear effects in the left cerebral hemisphere than the right.

Functional regression of thinking processes promotes prevalence of figurative thinking and activates attributive projectivity of thinking. Hypnotic reproduction of sensations and images involves attributive projectivity and reflects entirely personal traits and states and body functioning; this opens a way for projective transformations of problems and symptoms of psychogenic and somatic disorders. In the waking state, phenomenal models of the world and the self, stored in the subject’s memory, are superimposed on the current perception of the external world and the perception of self. In hypnosis subject’s phenomenal models of the world and the self are superimposed, projected on the limited self-perception, which leads to the formation of limited (intra-perceptual) hypnotic reality and expanded (intra-/extra-perceptual) hypnotic reality. All the phenomenal content of consciousness of the subject in hypnosis deeply and fully reflected his current psychological and bodily condition.

2.3 Biological component

Hypnotization generates hypnogenic stress. Hypnotherapy activates the systemic readaptation processes that are reflected in changes in neurohormonal and neurotransmitter secretions; activities of the immunological system; activation of protein, bilirubin, and cholesterol exchange; etc.

Hypnotherapy activates protein metabolism and activity of several enzyme systems of the organism. Hypnotherapy has a positive influence on the metabolism of bilirubin. The activation of cholesterol metabolism, characterized by a significant reduction of its concentration in the blood, has a significant clinical importance. The observed decrease of cholesterol concentration in blood, normalizing its metabolism in the process of hypnotherapy, means the restoration of activity of cell membranes, cells, organs, and tissues, slowing down their aging.

The stressful nature of hypnosis limits its therapeutic application, in that excessive intensity of hypnogenic stress may result in the maladaptation. Prolonged hypnotherapy may actually decrease and exhaust adaptable resources of an organism.

Hypnosis in clinical situations enables the possibility of a spontaneous (without specific suggestions) change of pain sensations.

In the 1980s during the course of group hypnotherapy in a therapeutic clinic, based on the universal hypnotherapy (UH) technique [10, 11, 17], which has no analgesic suggestions (see below), the author was faced with cases of spontaneous relief of acute (traumatic) pain after the session and opposite cases of the causeless appearance and amplification of patients' bodily pain during a hypnotherapeutic session, with its subsequent reduction in chronic disorders. Repeated cases of spontaneous modulation in hypnosis of pain in cases of acute and chronic pathological processes required explanation; therefore, using a special questionnaire, all such cases were studied. Over the 5 years of observation, the hypnotherapeutic dynamics of pain in acute traumas (15 patients) and in chronic pathological processes (mainly neurointoxications—167 patients) was studied. This study was clinical-phenomenological; the dynamics of the severity of pain were correlated with the results of other objectivizing methods of clinical research and the conclusions of relevant specialists. Data ware obtained on patients who received accidental injuries or dental care (bone fractures, sprains, tooth extraction) during an intensive short-term hypnotherapy of anxiety disorders (10–12 1-h sessions 3–5 times a week). The phenomenon of spontaneous hypnotic nociception became an unexpected, but regularly repeated, finding. Therefore, the question is not in the existence of the phenomenon of spontaneous hypnotic nociception but in the scientific understanding of its mechanisms.

The author's explanation of the phenomenon of spontaneous hypnotic nociception was based on the model of the structure and function of the nociceptive and vegetative regulation systems [20], according to which the pain impulse on the way from the pathological zone to the cerebral cortex can be damped by the damping system of the brain at three levels (spinal cord, thalamus, cerebral cortex), with the parallel activation of the hierarchical system of vegetative regulation of the pathological zone; this model satisfactorily explains the phenomenon of spontaneous hypnotic nociception [10, 11].

Western hypnology in the last 70 years in its development has paid a considerable attention to the research and practice of suggestive hypnotic analgesia. Researchers in experiment and practice have always been interested in only directed hypno-suggestive analgesia and its mechanisms, which essentially brought the phenomenon of spontaneous hypnotic nociception beyond the scope of any analysis.

It should be noted that studies of hypnotic analgesia have become the cornerstone in the development of modern hypnology, since after a long discussion they have led to the recognition that hypnosis is an altered state of consciousness [21–26]. Brain mechanisms underlying the modulation of pain perception under hypnotic conditions involve cortical as well as subcortical areas including anterior cingulate and prefrontal cortices, basal ganglia, and thalami [21]. It is demonstrated that hypnotic analgesia is characterized by a loss of coherence between the brain areas, reflecting "an alteration or even a breakdown of communication between the subunits of the brain" [20, 23, 24, 26]. Recently, in addition to experimental neurophysiological studies of the differences in the brain mechanisms of pain perception by high and low hypnotizable [27], analogous genetic studies have appeared [28]. Due to these studies, it became known that hypnotic assessment may predict lower responsiveness to opioids, and inefficient opioid system may be a distinctive characteristic of highs [29], and modulation of hypnotic pain responses is connected with differential recruitment of right prefrontal regions, which are involved in selective attention and inhibitory control [27].

Returning to the phenomenology of spontaneous nociceptive sensations in hypnotherapy, we need to note that it is characterized by the following features.

Acute pathological processes are characterized by one-step regressive dynamics of hypnotic nociception.

Chronic pathological processes are characterized by two-stage dynamics, including consistently associated progressive and regressive stages. The progressive stage of the dynamics of nociceptive sensations is observed at the beginning of hypnotherapy. At this stage, the strengthening or the appearance of nociceptive sensations in the area of localization of chronic pathological process occurs. On the regressive stage, the weakening or disappearance of nociceptive sensations caused by a chronic pathological process occurs.

The dynamics of the hypnotic nociception in acute and chronic pathological processes turns on spontaneously and has a positive therapeutic vector, being determined by the hypnogenic mechanism of readaptation. It can be strengthened by specific hypnotic suggestions.

2.4 Communicative component

Hypnotization and hypnotherapy can be considered as a goal-oriented communication—the communicative process. The hypnotic communicative process includes two basic components: cultural and interpersonal. The cultural component determines the varying boundaries, volumes, dynamics, and potential effectiveness of hypnotherapy while the interpersonal its specific implementation. The cultural and interpersonal components of hypnotherapy interact typologically, since culture defines historically determined patterns—communication styles that actualize the style sets of cultural and interpersonal components. Communicative styles, formed in the space of everyday communication, are then transferred to hypnotherapy, acquiring specialized features. The historical evolution of cultural communicative styles will generate the evolution of communicative styles of hypnotherapy. However, "within" hypnotherapy, a change in communicative styles will be perceived as an independent, personified process. The evolution of hypno-communication develops from classical and directive to non-directive hypnosis. In Russia, the style of universal hypnotherapy [29, 30] further appeared.

Directive hypnosis is a product of the European nineteenth century, with its class-hierarchical communicative style. Therefore, its communicative, being dominantly authoritarian, is based on the idea of direct "guiding" of "hypnable" patient by the hypnotherapist to a positive therapeutic result.

Non-directive hypnosis appeared in the 1970s, during the cultural heyday of individual rights and freedoms, with a manipulative management style in society. Its communicative style (Erickson's model) is based on the verbal, non-directive, and manipulative management of the patient, taking into account his or her non-verbal reactions, which uses non-directive adjustment and management, and on the idea of finding an adequate use of the resources of the wise unconscious, which uses thematic metaphors and descriptions, as tools for accessing resources.

The communicative style of universal hypnotherapy is built on a biopsychosocial paradigm; takes into account and rebuilds relevant cultural representations about hypnosis in the interests of therapy; uses primary positive cognitive-behavioral models and biological mechanisms of hypnotherapy; actively applies the non-verbal component of communicative interaction during hypnotherapy; attracts and potentiates the patient's recovery activity during the session and the entire course of hypnotherapy; and contributes to the formation of semantic therapeutic, aimed at active recovery and improvement.

A real hypno-communication is inevitably wider and deeper than the prescribed methodological frameworks. But the communicative style forms a therapeutic "core" that determines the initial selectivity, process, and the results of hypnotherapy. **Table 1** compares the communicative styles of directive, non-directive hypnosis and universal hypnotherapy.

Feature	Directive hypnosis	Non-directive hypnosis	Universal hypnotherapy
The conscious use of cultural representations about hypnosis	No	No	Yes
The use of cultural beliefs about hypnosis	Yes	Yes	No
Therapeutic transformation of cultural beliefs about hypnosis	No	No	Yes
Features of verbal communication	Spelling out prescriptive text	Algorithm of non-directive adjustment, management taking into account the trance microdynamics	Stimulation of positive directed activity of the patient using feedbacks
Non-verbal communication	Spontaneous use to support directive management	Mirroring and management reflecting the trance microdynamics	Active semantically directed use of non-verbal feedback channel
The ratio of activity of the therapist and patient	The dominant activity of the therapist	Reliance on the client's internal activity to utilize the resources of the unconscious with the dual activity of a therapist in realization of a client's and his own trance	Stimulation of the patient's increasing motivational activity during therapy with the creation of a semantic therapeutic space
Using of feedbacks	Intuitive, for the regulation of directive management	Conscious feedback in the form of adjusting and maintaining tracking mimic reactions, breathing, muscle tone, body postures, with reduced ideomotor feedback	Hypnotization, dehypnotization, body-oriented work is completely built on the feedback of verbal and non-verbal levels
Goal setting	Local restrictions overcoming by suggestion of alternative positive states, positive conditioning	Patient's access to the wise unconscious, its unlimited resources for problems solving + partial use of the principles of the "classical" approach	Stimulation of the patient's active assimilation of the basic positive mechanisms of healthy mental homeostasis
Therapy limitations	Non-hypnability, hypomania	Hypnosis resistance	Therapy cessation

Table 1.
Communicative styles of directive, non-directive hypnosis and universal hypnotherapy.

2.5 Outcomes of the integrative theory of hypnosis and hypnotherapy

Thus, hypnotherapy should be considered as a systemic therapeutic space, which includes four components: a culture-dependent communicative, defining the communicative style of hypnosis and hypnotherapy, which, as a rule, is attributed to the nature of hypnosis; the methodological component; the biological component of hypnosis, with neurobiological, analgesic, and general adaptive effects; and the component of the patient's personal response to the disorder and its therapy.

The regressive rearrangement of brain functioning to a prepubertal level, caused by hypnosis, sharply increases the subject's learning ability and the assimilation of suggestive therapeutically significant information.

The biological effects of hypnotherapy provide broader prospects for its clinical application. The therapeutic effectiveness of hypnotherapy is restricted by the presence and volume of stress-readaptive resources of the subject's organism and psyche. Technically, "correctness" of hypnotherapy is important, but it is not the only condition for treatment success. The absence or reduction of the hypnotherapy biological effect should be expected in patients undergoing a long-term treatment with adrenal hormonal medications and cases when the medication blocks or reduces the hypnotherapy biological readaptation effect (antidepressants, tranquilizers).

The integrative theory of hypnosis and hypnotherapy focuses on the basic systemic mechanisms of hypnosis and hypnotherapy, available for verification and concretization. Therefore, the constant accumulation of hypnosis research data (e.g., 3–9, 13, 14) will rather complement and expand its basic positions.

Thus, the default mode network—a large neural structure connecting different parts of the brain—was recently described [28, 31, 32]; its function is to provide a high level of activity even when the person is not engaged in a focused mental work. Recent experiments have described an increase in activity and an increase in the volume of the default mode network when practicing mindfulness meditation [33] and yoga [34].

According to the integrative theory of hypnosis and hypnotherapy, hypnosis development results in the reorganization of the brain activation system functioning from distribution to generation of activity. It was supposed that the functions of distribution and generation of activity need to be realized by morphologically different structures of the brain. So, the proposed system of activation generation of the brain activation system now is determined as a default mode network.

3. The method of universal hypnotherapy

More than three decades ago, the author developed a new method called universal hypnotherapy, so named because of its efficacy in both individual and group forms of therapy for a wide range of anxiety disorders [10, 11, 16, 23, 30, 35–39]. UH is rooted in the traditions of the Russian school of hypnotherapy, which shares its basic principles with positive approach (concept of resilience and resourcefulness) [29, 30] and mindfulness-based psychotherapeutic methods.

The author understands mental health and mental stability as an active adaptive state and process, which are spontaneously and actively maintained [16], whereas anxiety disorders break down the psyche's natural homeostasis. On the basis of research of therapy outcomes, we had described a model of the Personal System of Psychological Adaptation (PSPA) [11, 16, 29, 30, 40]. PSPA is a spontaneously activated homeostatic dynamic structure which forms during ontogenesis and creates a hierarchy of adaptive mechanisms from the earliest, most simple types to mature, complex, individualized, and personal ones which can be used as coping mechanisms. The hierarchic PSPA can be represented as a spherical multilayered model involving the following components: (1) a concentric structure of layers-levels of the hierarchic organization of adaptation mechanisms that form an expanding sphere around a "center" or the "self," the self who decides which outer layers will be predominantly activated; (2) a system of connections between each of layers-levels of the sphere; and (3) the highest mature level of the hierarchy of multilayer level mechanisms of psychological adaptation that has the capability of transforming the interactions between the underlying levels.

PSPA dynamics may express themselves in regressive, reactivating, or progressive (forming) transformations. In the case of regressive dynamics, the underlying levels, ontogenetically antecedent to it, become primarily active and assume the role of regulatory functions overriding more advanced functions; this results in the reorganization of the system of radial and spherical connections and development of new clusters not present at the previous stages of PSPA ontogenesis. Reactivation dynamics involves the reconstruction of the function initially of the top layer level of psychological adaptations and of PSPA "normal functioning" which has been disturbed by its previous regressive dynamics. The formation of PSPA dynamics is possible through the development of a higher layer level which would overcome the insufficiency and defectiveness of previous psychological adaptations of underlying levels. In cases of anxious maladaptation, weakening in the higher level of adaptive mechanisms causes the lower level of adaptive mechanisms to acquire greater behavioral significance. According to our model [11, 16, 21, 29, 38], psychotherapeutic interventions are especially suitable for cases of anxiety disorders in which there is a regressive activation of early ontogenic adaptation mechanisms.

Our empirical research on hypnotherapy outcomes [10, 11, 16, 29] has revealed that the dynamics in cases of efficient hypnotherapy with complete improvement in anxiety disorders is consistent with the mechanism of reactivation and, for organic disorders, with the mechanism of PSPA formation; in cases of partial improvement, the psychological dynamics for anxious disorders corresponds to PSPA incomplete reactivation, and for organic disorders it corresponds to PSPA incomplete formation.

3.1 Basic principles of universal hypnotherapy

UH method is based [10, 11, 16, 29, 30, 35–37, 39–41] on the activation of hypnotherapy biological healing potential leading to readaptation and to physiological and psychological self-regulation; more specifically, this includes stimulation of positive personal states and values and further depends on an individual's holistic positive engagement in recovery and in future steady adaptation. This process should lead to the creation of a positive goal-oriented semantic field enabling clients to act on hypnotic suggestions which should shape positive behaviors and therapeutic transformations.

UH is built on positive stimulation of patient's self-holistic activity all over hypnosis session: from hypnosis induction to therapy and final dehypnotization.

The specific techniques include distancing from stressogenic experiences and negative states, along with utilizing projective transformations and visualization of color. One of the most important hypnotherapeutic goals refers to the stimulation of a holistic personal positive activity that would promote recovery and future steady adaptation. In this respect, the strength of a patient's motivation to recover and to improve his or her state has a direct impact on the outcome. That is why stimulation of positive therapeutic motivation (PTM) to improve one's condition and to recover is considered, in universal hypnotherapy, to be its main therapeutic objective. Work with a patient's PTM starts on the first diagnostic session and becomes the foundation of the therapeutic contract; such motivation is maintained during the course of therapy and is acknowledged when the course is finished.

During the diagnostic session, after discussing the clinical diagnosis and possible prognosis of therapy and establishing a confidential relationship, a patient's motivation and wish to recover and/or to actively achieve the desired psychotherapeutic outcome are reviewed. Motivation for improvement, or for recovery, is directly or indirectly stimulated and maintained during the course of subsequent therapy, both within and outside of the hypnotherapy format. Indirect stimulation of the PTM is maintained by continuous encouragement of the patient's activity within the course of therapy, but also directly during the sessions of UH at all its stages.

Positive dynamics, commencing with the hypnotic induction, can be enhanced by showing the patient changes in symptoms, from session to session, based on a self-evaluation utilizing a graphic linear scale (ranging from the most negative to the most positive state); this allows for a comparison of results between sessions and identification of interim and general dynamics. Any increase in a patient's motivation for recovery and its behavioral manifestations is acknowledged and emphasized, during and at the end of therapy, as his or her tangible achievement in the process of positive adaptation. Furthermore, hypnosis is used to facilitate change.

Our understanding of hypnosis is that it leads to functionally regressive stages in brain functioning that trigger prepubertal imaginative thinking [10, 11, 29, 30] and promotes the reverse transformation in a regulatory hierarchy in which the meaning of words dominates over feelings, mental states, and perceptual experiences. Such a reorganization makes it possible in hypnosis to elicit actual feelings and mental states which could be utilized for positive transformation (i.e., confidence, calmness, freedom, self-efficiency and self-sufficiency, etc.) enabling the patient to experience positive personal states and values.

One of the most effective technique in dealing with specific symptoms includes somatic projective catharsis which requires awareness of personal control and limitations, along with the recognition of positive change in a person's condition, even though it may not be consciously known how it was achieved. The highest level of conscious differentiation occurs in the visual domain; it is less in the auditory and even less in the proprioceptive modalities [10, 11, 38, 39].

From a practical clinical perspective, catharsis is achieved after a client is informed that the perception of any event in one domain may also be reflected in another perceptual domain. Subsequently, it is proposed to the patient to become aware of anything unpleasant, negative, and painful that is a result from past experiences—memories, feelings, and also any feelings in his or her breast (i.e., heaviness or tension which occurs when a person is offended or derogated); if a person begins experiencing such a feeling, it is suggested to him or her to breathe it out. When after some attempts, the unpleasant feeling is diminished and each subsequent inhaling becomes easier, it is suggested that also the remaining part of the feeling can be breathed out. Breathing out the unpleasant sensation (i.e., heaviness or tension) is assigned to a client as a task to be carried out independently and to be continued until the maximum liberation from this unpleasant feeling is obtained, which is typically associated with a sense of peace.

Yet another technique utilizes visualization. The author's research [10, 11, 41] into the impact of color sensations and images induced in hypnosis was a stimulus for its integration with hypnotherapy for anxiety disorders. We have experimentally shown [10, 11, 37] that for the purposes of relaxation, the imaging of a blue color is the most suitable approach. That is why repeated blue color induction (with an interval of 1–2 minutes) is used during hypnotherapy sessions for the creation of a color-relaxing background to accompany the verbal suggestions.

Experimental data has shown that in mild and deep hypnosis, color inductions have a direct psycho-vegetative and emotional impact on a human being, and this impact is different from the one in the waking state because of the intensification of the activating potential of colors and the reduction of their sedative effect. The visualization of colors, induced in hypnosis, is accompanied by three phenomena of a neurophysiologic and psychological nature. The first one is achromatic transformation, when following hypnotic suggestion, chromatic colors (blue, green, yellow, red) are seen as achromatic (i.e., gray, black, brown). According to our experimental and clinical investigations, achromatic transformation phenomenon is the manifestation of a low level of activity of the reticular formation which is the brain activating system [10, 11, 41]. We should note that achromatic transformation is clinically significant; specifically, induced color visualization is restored as the patient's condition clinically improves [10, 11, 41]. The third phenomenon—chromatic transformation of colors induced in hypnosis—manifests as the recognition of another color, not the one which was suggested to the patient to be imagined. According to our data, the phenomenon of chromatic transformation of visualized color is conditional on an individual's personal characteristics associated with personal maturity. Therefore, the phenomenon of induced color chromatic transformation which is typically observed in children is reduced in healthy adults, but is increased in dissociative and somatoform disorders.

The phenomenology of induced color characterizes the depth of hypnosis; in mild hypnosis, visualized color is flat (two-dimensional) and changes sinusoidally; in deep hypnosis, it becomes three-dimensional and remains stable (in both healthy and emotionally disordered people).

The mind's ability to dissociate can be utilized for distancing from stressogenic experiences. It has been shown in psychological research [36, 42] that people's normal experiences proceed through subjective separation or distancing from the events, without cognitive distortion of their essence. Pathological attempts at psychological adaptation lead to events of the past events being confounded by cognitive deformations and distortions of events. Already more than 30 years ago, we noted that hypnotherapy allows for the normal experiencing of events and for subjective distancing while eliminating pathological adaptation mechanisms that distort the experience [3, 4]. To normalize the process of experiencing, we have elaborated a method of two-stage distancing with respect to current and past events; the first step serves for distancing from the current personally stressogenic events, and the second step is designed for distancing and resolving past stressogenic, negative, and traumatic experiences.

The mechanism of normal experiencing of current events presents the basic mechanism for the stable functioning of a healthy psyche; therefore, the author considers the sustainable inclusion of this mechanism in anxiety disorders as a key point in successful therapy. During UH the patient gains the ability to stably distance himself both from the current experiences and their projections into the future and from the past experiences.

Since the 1980s cognitive-behavioral therapy (CBT) has developed techniques based on modifications of ancient Vipassana meditation [43–48]: mindfulness-based stress reduction (MBSR) [49, 50] and mindfulness-based cognitive therapy (MBCT) [51, 52]. These techniques, producing "the third wave" of CBT evolution, have expanded the range of therapeutic efficacy for anxiety disorders, including generalized anxiety disorder (GAD) [53, 54].

Since these techniques also use the principle of distance experiencing, the author with the co-worker performed a comparative analysis of UH and CBT mindfulness-based techniques [36, 37], which revealed a significant similarity, consisting of (1) the formation of distancing, metaposition, and positive perception and (2) stimulation of personal integration and self-identity and working with body control and breathing control. UH and mindfulness-based techniques differ in parameter of experiences without judgment, duration of therapy, the need for meditation, and self-hypnosis after the end of therapy. UH explores only the principle of distancing, out of religious-philosophical connotations, it is the most short-term (10–15, rarely up to 20 sessions), and it does not require the continuation of self-hypnosis.

Yet another technique uses an individual's abilities to generate bodily sensations. Indirect suggestions of feelings of warmth (mostly) and coolness (in some areas of the body) are used for projective body work in universal hypnotherapy. Areas chosen for suggestion of warmth are the parieto-occipital zone with projection "inside head," posterior surface of the neck, shoulders, area of the left half of the breast (from the front), precostal space, and epigastria; suggestion of coolness while inhaling is directed to the nose, temples, and the zones, where it is needed. These suggestions establish experiences of warmth and coolness in the body which replace other less pleasant feelings.

The process of normalization requires restoration of restful sleep. That is why increasing the quality of sleep is one of the objectives of UH in which suggestion refers to the positive phenomenological model of restful sleep (falling asleep in the evening and in the morning waking up without remembering sleeping itself).

Before finishing the session of universal hypnotherapy, the therapist needs to seed suggestions about positive feelings taking place in the following order: body comfort, lucidity of thinking, and a good mood state.

3.2 Structure of session

A session of UH lasts for about 35–40 min, which includes (1) hypnosis induction and four (2–5) therapeutic parts.

3.3 Hypnosis induction in universal hypnotherapy

Hypnosis induction in UH is completely based on the realization of motivational activity of the hypnotized person, in the algorithm of bodily feedback with himself and implements the scheme: the hypnotized person is focusing on the desire to enter into hypnosis, mentally saying the phrase: "I want to enter into hypnosis," being ready (if the phrase dominates the person's mind for 20–30 s), giving the signal by raising any hand. The therapist touches the brush, suggesting that if the hand is spontaneously lowered, there happens a transition to hypnosis; the completion of the movement means the completion of the hypnotization. The therapist in immediate feedback briefly describes the characteristics of the movement of the hand and the behavior of the hypnotized, who perceives this as therapist's control of the induced movement.

The given method of hypnosis induction is contrary to cultural beliefs about hypnosis. Therefore, before the first induction, the therapist implements a special connecting script, which transforms the cultural model of hypnosis and allows the hypnotized person to accept fully the proposed method. It is effective in the vast majority of therapy-motivated patients (more than 99%), which allows patients in single and group format to enter hypnotic trance quickly and deeply.

The first part of UH therapeutic session is focused on somatic projective catharsis, whereas the second part of UH session consists of the following steps:

1. The induction of blue color, which is then repeated periodically with an interval of 1–2 min during the whole session

2. The enhancement of positive mental states and values

3. A two-step procedure of distancing from stressogenic experiences and resolving negative states or disorders and developing hypnotic self-suggestions that would shape positive behavior

4. The suggestion of sleep normalization

The third part of the session is represented by body projective work with a periodic induction of blue color. The fourth part of the session basically corresponds to its first part (but does not use projective "breathing"), and additionally the need to continue with modeling positive states is emphasized along with enhancing the positive dynamic and motivation for recovery.

So, the first and the third parts in the composition of the UH session focus on body projective working, using breathing techniques and inducement of pleasant feelings of warmth and coolness; it also emphasizes a personal activity and a personal responsibility to continue the work in the same manner. The goals of body projective work are liberation from symptom, normalization of functioning, and relaxation.

The second and third parts of the session actualize the feelings—states of confidence, calmness, and freedom; they also focus on distancing from stressogenic experiences and on resolution of negative states or disorders, with the development of positive behavioral models that would offer an alternative for pathological behavior and provide suggestions for sleep normalization.

The therapeutic influence on the client is achieved by providing a meaningful sensory stimulation through three channels (verbal, visual, and proprioceptive): active positive modeling of problem situations; repeating semantically significant components of the script which may be presented in the archaic folk song style —couplet-refrain—with induction of blue color as being the refrain; and presenting suggestions with the proper speech intonation.

UH has an integrated and focused content of the suggestions that support each other; as a result, regardless of whether a single individual component of therapy is effective, the whole therapeutic structure remains considerably efficient. UH creates a system of multilevel impacts stimulating a patient to assimilate actively his or her primary ideas, mental states, and experiences; its positive cognitive-behavioral models could be later implemented in real life, in order to eliminate psychopathology and to promote effective problem-solving. The application of UH creates a positive therapeutic semantic field and a goal-oriented therapeutic process.

At the end of the hypnotic session, the patient is informed about the upcoming dehypnotization according to a feedback scheme: a spontaneous return movement of a previously lowered hand is suggested, and when the hand returns to its initial position, the session is finished. The rate of dehypnotization is determined by the hypnotized person.

4. Universal hypnotherapy in the controlled therapy of anxiety disorders

The last two decades have become a time of significant increase in AD.

In the 2000s, the author applied UH for the treatment of panic disorder (PD) and GAD, adding a psycho-educational component to the therapy complex determined initially as a cognitive-oriented psychotherapy, later named by author positive-dialogue psychotherapy (PDP) for anxiety disorders. PDP has demonstrated sufficient clinical efficacy in the treatment of anxiety disorders (PD, GAD). In 2010, the author with the co-worker [35] conducted a controlled study of the effectiveness of PDP for anxiety disorders. Assuming a partial similarity of UH to mindfulness-based CBT methods, the study used additional psychometric estimation of mindfulness effect.

4.1 Method

4.1.1 Participants

Patients were recruited through an Internet advertisement on the site of Moscow Research Institute of Psychiatry soliciting for individuals with anxiety symptoms and panic attacks (PA) to take part in a clinical study of psychotherapeutic treatment of anxiety disorders. Psychotherapeutic treatment was offered for free. Inclusion criteria were that patients: (1) be between 18 and 60 years and (2) fulfill diagnostic criteria for either PD or GAD. Exclusion criteria were: (1) suicidality, (2) other psychiatric disorders as a primary diagnosis (schizophrenia spectrum disorders, affective disorders, personality disorders), (3) severe somatic diseases in the decompensation stage, and (4) parallel participation in other psychotherapeutic programs.

These criteria allowed for the presence of isolated comorbid depressive and phobic symptoms, provided that patients had AD as a primary diagnosis. Patients with initial pharmacological treatment (antidepressants, anxiolytics, tranquilizers) were also included in the study. The possibility of termination of pharmacological treatment as their state improves during the therapy was discussed with such patients. The pharmacological treatment was terminated at all patients after 5–6 psychotherapeutic sessions. **Figure 5** illustrates the patient flow in the study.

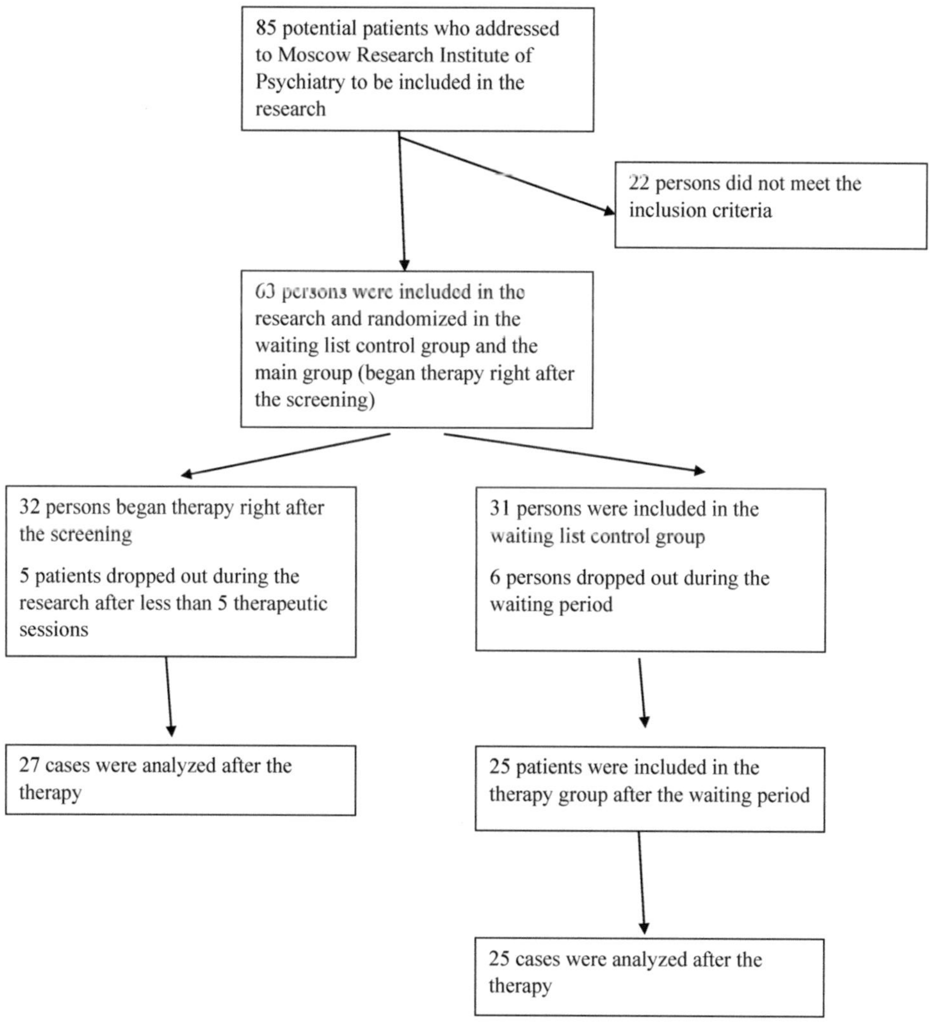

Figure 5.
Research design.

4.1.2 Procedures

After a preliminary telephone screening, eligible participants (N = 63) were invited for a structural clinical interview based on the criteria of the research version of ICD-10 [10]. Participants also completed a number of self-reported questionnaires for baseline assessment.

4.1.3 Design

After diagnostic evaluation and completion of all questionnaires, patients were randomly assigned to a treatment group or a waiting-list group. In the treatment group, patients went in therapy immediately and completed the self-report questionnaires at the end of the therapeutic process. Patients on a control waiting-list group were informed about a certain order for the beginning of the therapy and that they had to complete the questionnaires two times (the second time was 3 weeks after the first). The evaluation of psychometric data of this group was carried out 3 weeks before the treatment, just before the start of treatment and at the end of treatment. The control waiting-list group was a control group for itself and for the first group.

4.2 Treatment

PDP is based on the protocol developed by the author [14, 15]. The therapeutic intervention consists of three main components: (1) psycho-educational; (2) causal cognitive-orientated; and (3) hypnotherapeutic.

The psycho-education component includes a didactic material covering the following information about: (1) anxiety as a normal reaction of mobilization, needed to cope or avoid a dangerous situation; (2) anxiety disorder and the phases of its development for PD and GAD, because of the "swinging" of anxiety reaction by a combination of social, biological, and psychogenic factors; and (3) possibilities of psychotherapeutic treatment of AD based on (a) the resolution of current psychogenic issues, (b) the excluding intoxicating mechanisms (if there are any), (c) the coping with phobic component (if it's present), (d) the general increase of adaptive resources of the organism (through lifestyle rationalization), and (e) the normalization of vegetative regulation by psychotherapy or combination of psychotherapy with pharmacotherapy. The psycho-educational component of PDP is realized during the first therapy session, in an individual or group format.

The causal cognitive-orientated component of PDP has the following objectives: (1) Individual assimilation of the psycho-educational component. (2) Normalization of patient's traumatic experiences during a PA (if there are any). (3) Stimulation of patient's coping of anxiety triggers, restrictive behaviors, and phobias. (4) Stimulation of a healthy lifestyle with normalization of vegetative regulation. (5) Development of patient's autonomous understanding and coping with problem situations. (6) Development of skills of positive thinking and attitude.

The causal cognitive-orientated component of PDP is used during 2–7 sessions for about 20 min.

The hypnotherapeutic component of PDP uses the method of UH [10, 11, 29, 30, 36, 37, 39–41] which contains the following therapeutic interventions: (1) Increase of self-identity and self-integrity. (2) Transformation of patient's projections of his/her psychogenic and somatic-sensorial content. (3) Use of sedative and detachment influences of reproduced colors. (4) Stimulation of detachment of stress experience and completion of negative states and experiences based on modeling and realization of positive correct behavior. (5) Repeat of the interventions mentioned above

(1–4). (6) Creation in hypnotherapy a positive vector semantic space for patient's active therapeutic changes.

The UH, done in the second part of a 1-h session of PDP, lasts for 40 min. The frequency of PDP sessions is three times a week; the total number of sessions varies from 8 to 15 (till the stable improvement of patient's state).

4.3 Instruments

4.3.1 Psychometric instruments

The symptomatic questionnaire SCL-90-R is a Russian adaptation of N. Tarabarina [55]. In our research the following scales were used: DEP, depression; ANX, anxiety; and GSI, general severity index, a measure of the overall psychological distress. The Spielberger State-Trait Anxiety Inventory (STAI) is a Russian adaptation of Hanin [56]. The following tools were also used: Beck's depression inventory (BDI) [57]; Sheehan Clinical Anxiety Rating Scale (ShARS) [58]; and Five-Factor Mindfulness Questionnaire (FFMQ) [59], its short version. The FFMQ was adapted for Russian-speaking population by the authors. The Mindful Attention Awareness Scale (MAAS) [60] was adapted to Russian-speaking population by the authors.

4.3.2 Statistical instruments

The statistical analysis was made with the use of the program "Statistica 10." The following data were compared, using this program: (1) Initial data of the therapeutic group and the waiting-list control (WLC) group. (2) Initial data of the WLC group and the data of the WLC group at the beginning of the therapy. (3) Initial data of the primary therapeutic group and the WLC group at the point of the beginning of the therapy. (4) Initial and final data of the combined therapeutic group and the data from the WLC group (initial and at the point of the beginning of the therapy). (5) Initial and final data of the subgroup of monopsychotherapy (MPT) and the subgroup of psychotherapy with gradual discontinuation of psychopharmacotherapy (PT + PPT). (6) Initial and final data of the subgroup of PD and the subgroup of GAD.

Gender and demographic and psychometric characteristics were used in the statistical analysis. The methods of descriptive statistics (M, SD) and nonparametric statistics (Wilcoxon's test, Mann–Whitney test) were used. To evaluate the effect size, Cohen's unbiased d-index was used [61, 62] ($d \leq 0.20$, small effect size; $d \leq 0.50$, moderate effect size; $d \leq 0.80$, large effect size). The effect size was calculated using a pooled standard deviation. χ^2 was used to compare the degree of improvement between groups.

4.4 Results

4.4.1 Baseline characteristics of the main and control groups

Patients' gender and demographic and diagnostic characteristics are presented in **Tables 2** and **3**. Apart from the type of anxiety disorder, the presence of the accompanying psychopharmacotherapy at the beginning of the treatment was taken into consideration.

Twenty-nine participants (55.8%) were diagnosed with PD (11 of them were taking psychopharmacological medications at the beginning of the therapy); 23 participants (44.2%) had GAD as the main diagnosis (9 of them were taking

	Total (*n* = 52)		Primary therapeutic group (*n* = 27)		WLC group (*n* = 25)	
	n	%	*n*	%	*n*	%
Gender (female)	35	67.3	20	74.1	15	60.0
Age (*M*, SD)	31.6	10.4	30.9	9	32.5	12.1
Education						
High	41	78.8	20	74.1	21	84.0
Student	6	11.5	2	7.4	4	16.0
Vocational school	4	7.7	4	14.8		
Secondary school	1	1.9	1	3.7		
Marital status						
Married/partner	23	44.2	12	44.4	11	44.0
Single	27	51.9	15	55.6	12	48.0
Divorced	2	3.8			2	8.0
Diagnosis						
PD	29	55.8	16	59.3	13	52.0
GAD	23	44.2	11	40.7	12	48.0
Months science onset (*M*, SD)	54.5	77.4	51.5	53.7	58.4	100.8
PPT	20	38.5	12	44.4	8	32.0

Primary therapeutic group—group that began therapy right after the screening; WLC group—waiting list control group; PPT—number of subjects with psychopharmacotherapy.

Table 2.
Patient characteristics.

psychopharmacological medications at the beginning of the therapy). The basic clinical, demographic, and clinical-psychometric criteria of the main and control groups were compared using the Mann–Whitney test and χ^2 test for independent samples. The two groups did not show significant differences in all the parameters, but STAI-S score (which was significantly different in the groups of MPT and PT + PPT ($p = 0.01$)) and SCL-90 ANX ($p = 0.03$) and ShARS ($p = 0.007$) scores were significantly different in the PD and GAD groups (**Tables 1** and **2**). That fact witnesses a general success of the randomization.

The duration of the illness till the moment of the beginning of the treatment was also significantly different in the groups of MPT and PT + PPT (18.1 months and 112.8 months, accordingly; $p < 0.0001$). The mean duration of psychopharmacotherapy before the treatment in the group PT + PPT was 37.6 months. In all these cases (except 2) during this period the patients received more than two different psychopharmacological courses. These data allow us to call the PT + PPT group a therapy-resistant group.

4.4.2 Patients in the therapy: dropped out patients and patients who finished the therapy

Eleven out of 63 patients (17%) dropped out before the end of the treatment. Four patients could not visit sessions due to time limitations, 7 patients dropped out without any explanation, and 52 patients finished the therapy. The mean duration of the therapeutic course for these patients was 13.5 sessions of PDP. However, in the MPT group, the mean number of sessions was 11.5, and in the PT + PPT group, this number was significantly higher—16.7 sessions ($p = 0.0005$).

DOI: http://dx.doi.org/10.5772/intechopen.92761

Scale	Total (n = 52)		Primary therapeutic group (n = 27)		WLC group at screening point (n = 25)		WLC group right before the therapy (n = 25)		MPT group (n = 32)		PT + PPT group (n = 20)		PD group (n = 29)		GAD group (n = 23)	
	M	SD	*M*	SD	*M*	SD	*M*	SD	*M*	SD	*M*	SD	*M*	SD	*M*	SD
SCL-90 DEP	1.66	0.82	1.58	0.75	1.59	0.81	1.74	0.90	1.56	0.64	1.81	1.06	1.68	0.77	1.62	0.91
SCL-90 ANX	1.85	0.93	1.75	0.87	1.75	0.89	1.96	1.00	1.76	0.80	2.01	1.11	2.09	0.81	1.54[2]	1.00
SCL-90 GSI	1.29	0.62	1.23	0.66	1.33	0.58	1.35	0.58	1.21	0.41	1.42	0.86	1.40	0.62	1.14	0.61
STAI-S	37.35	11.11	38.59	10.25	36.16	11.12	36.00	12.04	34.25	6.66	42.30[1]	14.74	36.80	10.83	38.09	11.71
STAI-T	55.08	9.79	54.63	9.86	53.72	6.71	55.56	9.90	52.69	8.10	58.90	11.19	55.53	10.12	54.45	9.52
BDI	19.54	10.24	19.96	10.74	19.80	10.20	19.08	9.87	18.44	8.92	21.30	12.09	19.93	10.89	19.00	9.49
ShARS	48.77	25.47	49.11	21.75	51.76	22.10	48.40	29.43	45.38	24.95	54.20	25.99	56.67	25.03	38.00[3]	22.37
FFMQ-SF	71.54	9.28	72.60	8.62	71.68	8.95	70.40	9.99	71.70	7.34	71.28	11.95	72.46	9.02	70.28	9.68
MAAS	3.90	0.72	3.97	0.76	3.87	0.70	3.82	0.68	3.85	0.75	3.97	0.67	3.97	0.82	3.79	0.55

SCL-90 DEP, ANX, GSI—depression, anxiety, and global severity index of symptom checklist 90; STAI-S—Spielberger Anxiety Inventory, state anxiety; STAI-T—Spielberger Anxiety Inventory, trait anxiety; BDI—Beck Depression Inventory; ShARS—Sheehan Clinical Anxiety Rating Scale; FFMQ-SF—Five-Factor Mindfulness Questionnaire, short version, total score; MAAS—Mindfulness Attention Awareness Scale; MPT group—monopsychotherapy group; PT + PPT group—psychotherapy + psychopharmacotherapy group with later psychopharmacotherapy withdrawal.
[1]*$p < 0.01$ (comparing to MPT group).*
[2]*$p < 0.03$ (comparing to PD group).*
[3]*$p < 0.007$ (comparing to PD group).*

Table 3.
Means and standard deviations at screening point and right before the therapy.

4.4.3 Psychotherapy results according to psychometric data

Psychotherapy results according to psychometric data are shown in **Tables 4–6**. The combined psychotherapy results are presented in **Table 4**. Comparing before and after data in the main group and analyzing these data in comparison with WLC group data, we can observe a significant decrease of all clinical scales' scores in the main group (SCL-90 DEP, SCL-90 ANX, SCL-90 GSI, STAI-S, STAI-T, BDI, ShARS) practically to the level of the nonclinical norm.

For the STAI-T scale, the effect size is moderate (0.73); for the other six clinical scales, the effect size is large (from 0.87 to 1.28). The mindfulness scores (FFMQ-SF, MAAS) increased significantly with large (FFMQ-SF = 0.98) and moderate (MAAS = 0.71) effect sizes. There were no such changes in the WLC group during 3 weeks of waiting period.

Psychotherapy results in the PD and GAD groups are shown in **Table 5**. Significant changes of all clinical scales' scores are observed in both groups. There were no statistically significant differences between the groups at the end of the therapy. The effect size for clinical scales (SCL-90 DEP, SCL-90 ANX, SCL-90 GSI, STAI-S, STAI-T, BDI, ShARS) was bigger in the PD group, in which for all the scales it was large (from 0.99 to 1.75), but moderate for STAI-T (0.69). In the GAD group, the effect size was moderate (from 0.53 to 0.74) for five scales (SCL-90 DEP, SCL-90 ANX, SCL-90 GSI, STAI-T, ShARS) and large (from 1.06 to 1.20) for two scales (STAI-S, BDI). Changes in mindfulness scores in the PD group were moderate (FFMQ-SF, 0.78; MAAS, 0.62); in the GAD group, the effect size was large for FFMQ-SF (1.20) and moderate for MAAS (0.61).

Results for the groups of MPT and psychotherapy with gradual withdrawal of psychopharmacotherapy (PT + PPT) are presented in **Table 6**. It is important to notice significant differences between MPT and PT + PPT groups at the end of the therapy according to six scales of 9 (SCL-90 DEP, SCL-90 ANX, ACL-90 GSI, STAI-S, STAI-T, ShARS), which is confirmed by a larger effect for the MPT group. Comparing before and after the scores in the MPT group, there is a significant decrease of all scales' scores to the level of the nonclinical norm (SCL-90 DEP, SCL-90 ANX, SCL-90 GSI, STAI-S, STAI-T, BDI, ShARS). For all seven scales, the effect size is large (from 1.13 to 1.91). Mindfulness scores increased significantly with large (FFMQ-SF = 1.17) and moderate (MAAS = 0.64) effect sizes.

Comparing before and after the data in the PT + PPT group, a moderate significant decrease was observed for six clinical scales' scores (SCL-90 ANX, SCL-90 GSI, STAI-S, STAI-T, BDI, ShARS). There were no significant changes in SCL-90 DEP scores. The effect sizes are large for three scales (STAI-S, 0.94; BDI, 0.84; ShARS, 1.11), moderate for one scale (SCL-90 ANX, 0.56), and weak for two scales (SCL-90 GSI, 0.39; STAI-T, 0.46). Mindfulness scores significantly increased with a moderate effect size (FFMQ-SF, 0.75; MAAS, 0.57).

Results of this controlled study show high effectiveness of PDP for PD and GAD, which is confirmed by mainly high or moderate size effects in psychometric data.

The correctness of distinction of the groups of MPT and PT + PPT is confirmed by statistical analysis of psychometric data. The effectiveness of MPT is significantly higher than the combination of PT + PPT, while the duration of MPT is significantly lower.

The use of instruments in this research for mindfulness evaluation (FFMQ-SF, MAAS) was justified, because for the first time the significant increase of these parameters (with moderate effect size) was shown for the UH (PDP). Additionally, the effectiveness of the PDP was compared with MBCT [53] and MBSR [54] methods for several psychometric clinical scales and mindfulness scales

Scale	Therapy group (n = 52)			Waiting list control group (n = 25)			
	M	SD	d (before-after)	*M*	SD	d (before-after)	d (between the groups)
SCL-90 DEP							
At baseline	1.66	0.82		1.59	0.81		
At the end of treatment	0.94[1]	0.83	0.87	1.74[2]	0.90	0.18	0.92
SCL-90 ANX							
At baseline	1.85	0.93		1.75	0.89		
At the end of treatment	0.93[1]	0.84	1.04	1.96[2]	1.00	0.22	1.12
SCL-90 GSI							
At baseline	1.29	0.62		1.33	0.58		
At the end of treatment	0.74[1]	0.59	0.89	1.35[2]	0.58	0.03	1.04
STAI-S							
At baseline	37.35	11.11		36.16	11.12		
At the end of treatment	24.81[1]	10.11	1.18	36.00[2]	12.04	0.01	1.01
STAI-T							
At baseline	55.08	9.79		53.72	6.71		
At the end of treatment	48.12[1]	9.27	0.73	55.56[3]	9.90	0.22	0.78
BDI							
At baseline	19.54	10.24		19.80	10.20		
At the end of treatment	9.65[1]	7.41	1.11	19.08[2]	9.87	0.07	1.08
ShARS							
At baseline	48.77	25.47		51.76	22.10		
At the end of treatment	22.04[1]	14.99	1.28	48.40[2]	29.43	0.13	1.13
FFMQ-SF							
At baseline	71.54	9.28		71.68	8.95		
At the end of treatment	80.12[1]	8.06	0.98	70.40[2]	9.99	0.13	1.07
MAAS							
At baseline	3.90	0.72		3.87	0.70		
At the end of treatment	4.35[1]	0.71	0.63	3.82[4]	0.68	0.07	0.76

SCL-90 DEP, ANX, GSI—depression, anxiety and global severity index of symptom checklist 90; STAI-S—Spielberger Anxiety Inventory, state anxiety; STAI-T—Spielberger Anxiety Inventory, trait anxiety; BDI—Beck Depression Inventory; ShARS—Sheehan Clinical Anxiety Rating Scale; FFMQ-SF—Five-Factor Mindfulness Questionnaire, short version, total score; MAAS—Mindfulness Attention Awareness Scale; MPT group—monopsychotherapy group; PT + PPT group—psychotherapy + psychopharmacotherapy group with later psychopharmacotherapy withdrawal.
[1]*$p < 0.0001$ (comparing to the baseline figures).*
[2]*$p \leq 0.0001$ (comparing to therapy group).*
[3]*$p < 0.001$ (comparing to therapy group).*
[4]*$p < 0.002$ (comparing to therapy group).*

Table 4.
Treatment effect.

(see **Table 7**), which demonstrated comparable effect sizes for the three methods. The received data expand the representation about mindfulness phenomenon, taking it beyond the boundaries of traditional meditation and bringing closer to the basic mechanisms of UH activation of the psychological process of normal coping by means of distancing.

Scale	PD group (*n* = 29)			GAD group (*n* = 23)			
	M	SD	d (before-after)	*M*	SD	d (before-after)	d (between the groups)
SCL-90 DEP							
At baseline	1.68	0.77		1.62	0.91		
At the end of treatment	0.82[1]	0.83	1.05	1.09[4]	0.83	0.59	0.33
SCL-90 ANX							
At baseline	2.09	0.81		1.54	1.00		
At the end of treatment	0.89[1]	0.72	1.52	0.98[3]	1.00	0.53	0.10
SCL-90 GSI							
At baseline	1.40	0.62		1.14	0.61		
At the end of treatment	0.72[1]	0.60	1.08	0.78[2]	0.59	0.57	0.10
STAI-S							
At baseline	36.80	10.83		38.09	11.71		
At the end of treatment	24.13[1]	9.77	1.20	25.72[3]	10.73	1.06	0.15
STAI-T							
At baseline	55.53	10.12		54.45	9.52		
At the end of treatment	48.20[1]	10.66	0.69	48.00[2]	7.20	0.74	0.02
BDI							
At baseline	19.93	10.89		19.00	9.49		
At the end of treatment	10.13[1]	8.29	0.99	9.00[2]	6.16	1.20	0.15
ShARS							
At baseline	56.67	25.03		38.00	22.37		
At the end of treatment	20.40[1]	13.78	1.75	24.27[3]	16.56	0.67	0.25
FFMQ-SF							
At baseline	72.46	9.02		70.28	9.68		
At the end of treatment	79.18[1]	8.17	0.78	81.32[3]	7.95	1.20	0.27
MAAS							
At baseline	3.97	0.82		3.79	0.55		
At the end of treatment	4.45[1]	0.70	0.62	4.20[3]	0.71	0.61	0.35

SCL-90 DEP, ANX, GSI—depression, anxiety and global severity index of symptom checklist 90; STAI-S—Spielberger Anxiety Inventory, state anxiety; STAI-T—Spielberger Anxiety Inventory, trait anxiety; BDI—Beck Depression Inventory; ShARS—Sheehan Clinical Anxiety Rating Scale; FFMQ-SF—Five-Factor Mindfulness Questionnaire, short version, total score; MAAS—Mindfulness Attention Awareness Scale; MPT group—monopsychotherapy group; PT + PPT group—psychotherapy + psychopharmacotherapy group with later psychopharmacotherapy withdrawal.
[1]*$p < 0.0001$ (comparing to baseline figures).*
[2]*$p < 0.001$ (comparing to baseline figures).*
[3]*$p < 0.005$ (comparing to baseline figures).*
[4]*$p < 0.02$ (comparing to baseline figures).*

Table 5.
Treatment results in PD and GAD groups.

4.4.4 Conclusion

1. PDP is clinically effective for the treatment of PD and GAD, comparing with the WLC group.

2. PDP is more effective in the MPT format than in PT + PPT format.

Scale	MPT group (n = 32)			PT + PPT group (n = 20)			
	M	SD	d (before-after)	M	SD	d (before-after)	d (between the groups)
SCL-90 DEP							
At baseline	1.56	0.64		1.81	1.06		
At the end of treatment	0.62[1]	0.45	1.67	1.45[6]	1.05	0.34	1.03
SCL-90 ANX							
At baseline	1.76	0.80		2.01	1.11		
At the end of treatment	0.66[1]	0.46	1.64	1.37[3,7]	1.11	0.56	0.84
SCL-90 GSI							
At baseline	1.21	0.41		1.42	0.86		
At the end of treatment	0.53[1]	0.25	1.91	1.08[4,7]	0.80	0.39	0.92
STAI-S							
At baseline	34.25	6.66		42.30	14.74		
At the end of treatment	22.00[1]	7.85	1.64	29.30[2,6]	11.81	0.94	0.73
STAI-T							
At baseline	52.69	8.10		58.90	11.19		
At the end of treatment	44.75[1]	5.32	1.13	53.50[3,5]	11.61	0.46	0.97
BDI							
At baseline	18.44	8.92		21.30	12.09		
At the end of treatment	8.44[1]	4.99	1.35	11.60[3]	10.02	0.84	0.40
ShARS							
At baseline	45.38	24.95		54.20	25.99		
At the end of treatment	18.38[1]	10.38	1.38	27.90[3,6]	19.19	1.11	0.62
FFMQ-SF							
At baseline	71.70	7.34		71.28	11.95		
At the end of treatment	80.60[1]	7.76	1.17	79.40[4]	8.65	0.75	0.15
MAAS							
At baseline	3.85	0.75		3.97	0.67		
At the end of treatment	4.31[1]	0.65	0.64	4.40[2]	0.80	0.57	0.12

SCL-90 DEP, ANX, GSI—depression, anxiety and global severity index of symptom checklist 90; STAI-S—Spielberger Anxiety Inventory, state anxiety; STAI-T—Spielberger Anxiety Inventory, trait anxiety; BDI—Beck Depression Inventory; ShARS—Sheehan Clinical Anxiety Rating Scale; FFMQ-SF—Five-Factor Mindfulness Questionnaire, short version, total score; MAAS—Mindfulness Attention Awareness Scale; MPT group—monopsychotherapy group. PT + PPT group—psychotherapy + psychopharmacotherapy group with later psychopharmacotherapy withdrawal.
[1] $p < 0.0001$ *(comparing to baseline figures).*
[2] $p < 0.001$ *(comparing to baseline figures).*
[3] $p < 0.005$ *(comparing to baseline figures).*
[4] $p < 0.01$ *(comparing to baseline figures).*
[5] $p < 0.001$ *(between the groups).*
[6] $p < 0.01$ *(between the groups).*
[7] $p < 0.05$ *(between the groups).*

Table 6.
Treatment results in MPT and PT + PPT groups.

3. PDP is effective in the PT + PPT format, so it can be used for a successful therapy on patients recurrent and resistant to PPT.

4. UH produces a distinct mindfulness effect comparable to that for mindfulness-based CBT.

Authors	Diagnosis	Intervention	No of subjects	Scales	M1	S1	M2	S2	D-unbiased
Evans and co-authors	GAD	MBCT	11	BDI	13.8	7.9	8.82	8.5	0.56
				MAAS	3.68	0.66	4.2	0.58	0.78
Vollestad and co-authors	AD	MBSR	31	BDI	17.3	9.3	8.5	9.1	0.93
				SCL-90 GSI	1.3	0.6	0.7	0.7	0.9
				FFMQ	113.8	21.6	128.2	22.3	0.64
Tukaev and Kuznetsov	GAD and PD	PDP (UH)	52	BDI	19.54	10.24	9.65	7.41	1.11
				SCL-90 ANX	1.85	0.93	0.93	0.84	1.04
				SCL-90 GSI	1.29	0.62	0.74	0.59	0.89
				SCL-90 DEP	1.66	0.82	0.94	0.83	0.87
				FFMQ	71.54	9.28	80.12	8.88	0.99
				MAAS	3.9	0.72	4.35	0.71	0.63

Table 7.
The comparison of PDP (UH) MBCT, MBSR efficiency, and mindfulness effect in therapy of anxiety disorders.

5. Chapter conclusion

In this chapter, the author attempted to describe briefly and systematically some of the results of his experimental, theoretical, and clinical studies in the field of hypnosis and hypnotherapy.

The integrative theory of hypnosis allows us to consistently explain a number of features of the hypnosis phenomenon related to hypnotization and analgesia, improving learning ability (suggestibility) and biological effects and providing a wide range of therapeutic applications and the evolution of the communicative style of hypnotherapy. The universal hypnotherapy presents the practical embodiment of the developed theoretical understanding of hypnosis, which in the controlled study has showed a high efficacy in the treatment of anxiety disorders.

The fact that UH, developed independently in the 1970s to 1980s of the twentieth century, was later assigned to the category of methods of positive psychology and psychotherapy, the author considers natural, associated with the fundamental prevailing of positive susceptibility of hypnotic (functional child) psyche. The therapeutically valuable feature of this technique is its pronounced mindfulness effect, which we explain as reactivated by therapy homeostatically significant mechanism of normal experiencing.

Author details

Rashit Tukaev
Department of Psychotherapy and Sexology, Russian Medical Academy of Continuous Professional Education, Ministry of Healthcare of the Russian Federation, Moscow, Russia

*Address all correspondence to: tukaevrd@gmail.com

References

[1] Bogdanov A, Galashina A, Kulikov M. Influence of "animal hypnosis" on intersignal rhythmic movement in defense dominant. I. P. Pavlov Journal of Higher Nervous Activity. 2007;**57**(2): 186-195 (in Russian)

[2] Galashina A, Kulikov M, Bogdanov A. Influence of "animal hypnosis" on rhythmic defensive dominance. Journal of Higher Nervous Activity. 2007;**57**(1):44-52 (in Russian)

[3] Tadić A, Victor A, Başkaya O, von Cube R, Hoch J, Kouti I, et al. Interaction between gene variants of the serotonin transporter promoter region (5-HTTLPR) and catechol O-methyltransferase (COMT) in borderline personality disorder. American Journal of Medical Genetics. Part B, Neuropsychiatric Genetics. 2009;**150B**(4):487-495

[4] Zinkstok J, van Nimwegen L, van Amelsvoort T, de Haan L, Yusuf MA, Baas F, et al. Catechol-O-methyltransferase gene and obsessive-compulsive symptoms in patients with recent-onset schizophrenia: Preliminary results. Psychiatry Research. 2008; **15**(1–3):1-8

[5] Szekely A, Kovacs-Nagy R, Bányai EI, Gosi-Greguss AC, Varga K, Halmai Z, et al. Association between hypnotizability and the catechol-O-methyltransferase (COMT) polymorphism. The International Journal of Clinical and Experimental Hypnosis. 2010;**58**(3):301-315

[6] Rominger C, Weiss EM, Nagl S, Niederstätter H, Parson W, Papousek I. Carriers of the COMT Met/Met allele have higher degrees of hypnotizability, provided that they have good attentional control: A case of gene-trait interaction. International Journal of Clinical and Experimental Hypnosis. 2014;**62**(4):455-482

[7] Katonai ER, Szekely A, Vereczkei A, Sasvari-Szekely M, Bányai ÉI, Varga K. Dopaminergic and serotonergic genotypes and the subjective experiences of hypnosis. The International Journal of Clinical and Experimental Hypnosis. 2017;**65**(4): 379-397

[8] Holdevici I, Crăciun B. Hypnosis in the treatment of patients with anxiety disorders. Procedia - Social and Behavioral Sciences. 2013;**78**:471-475

[9] Hettema JM, An S-S, Bukszar J, van den Oord EJCG, Neale MC, Kendler KS, et al. COMT contributes to genetic susceptibility shared among anxiety spectrum phenotypes. Biological Psychiatry. 2008;**64**(4): 302-310. DOI: 10.1016/j.biopsych.2008.03.014

[10] Tukaev R. Phenomenology and Biology of Hypnosis (Theoretical Analysis and Practical Application). Ufa: Gilem; 1996 (in Russian)

[11] Tukaev R. Hypnosis; Phenomenon and Clinical Application. Moscow: MIA; 2006 (in Russian)

[12] Bogdanov A, Galashina A, Tukaev R. The influence of "animal hypnosis" to transmission on neural networks of information about parameters of external stimulation caused by formed rhythmic defensive dominant. On the way to an evolutionary understanding of hypnosis. Psychiatry, Psychotherapy and Clinical Psychology. 2016;**7**(1):133-144 (in Russian)

[13] Kallio S, Koivisto M. Seeing blue as red: A hypnotic suggestion can alter visual awareness of colors. The International Journal of Clinical and Experimental Hypnosis. 2016;**64**(3): 261-284

[14] Koivisto M, Kirjanen S, Revonsuo A, Kallio S. A preconscious neural mechanism of hypnotically altered colors: A double case study. PLoS One. 2013;**8**(8):e70900

[15] Revonsuo A. Consciousness. The Science of Subjectivity. Vol. 1. New York, Hove: Psychology Press; 2010;(1). p. 352

[16] Tukaev RD. Psychotherapy: Structures and Mechanisms. Moscow: Medical Information Agency; 2007 (in Russian)

[17] Jasiukaitis P, Nouriani P, Hugdahi K, Spiegel D. Relateralizing hypnosis: Or, have we been barking up the wrong hemisphere? The International Journal of Clinical and Experimental Hypnosis. 1997;**45**(2):158-177

[18] Hoeft F, Gabrieli JD, Whitfield-Gabrieli S, Haas BW, Bammer R, Menon V, et al. Functional brain basis of hypnotizability. Archives of General Psychiatry. 2012;**69**(10):1064-1072

[19] Spiegel D. Tranceformations: Hypnosis in brain and body. Depression and Anxiety. 2013;**30**:342-352

[20] Ananin VF. Reflexology (Theory and Methods). Biomedinform. Moscow; RUDN Publishing House; 1992. p. 168 (in Russian)

[21] Vanhaudenhuyse A, Laureys S, Faymonville ME. Neurophysiology of hypnosis. Neurophysiologie Clinique. 2014;**44**(4):343-353

[22] Kallio S, Revonsuo A. Hypnotic phenomena and altered states of consciousness: A multilevel framework of description and explanation. Contemporary Hypnosis. 2003;**20**: 111-164

[23] De Pascalis V, Cacace I, Massicolle F. Perception and modulation of pain in waking and hypnosis: Functional significance of phase-ordered gamma oscillations. Pain. 2004; **112**:27-36

[24] De Pascalis V. Phase-ordered gamma oscillations and modulation of hypnotic experience. In: Jamieson GA, editor. Hypnosis and Conscious States: The Cognitive Neuroscience Perspective. Oxford: Oxford University Press; 2007. pp. 67-89

[25] Jamieson GA, Burgess AP. Hypnotic induction is followed by state-like changes in the organization of EEG functional connectivity in the theta and beta frequency bands in high-hypnotically susceptible individuals. Frontiers in Human Neuroscience. 2014; **8**:528

[26] Braboszcz C, Brandao-Farinelli E, Vuilleumier P. Hypnotic analgesia reduces brain responses to pain seen in others [published correction appears in Sci Rep. 2018 Nov 16;8(1):17220]. Scientific Reports. 2017;**7**(1):9778. DOI: 10.1038/s41598-017-10310-4

[27] Presciuttini S, Curcio M, Sciarrino R, Scatena F, Jensen MP, Santarcangelo EL. Polymorphism of opioid receptors μ1 in highly hypnotizable subjects. International Journal of Clinical and Experimental Hypnosis. 2018;**66**(1):106-118. DOI: 10.1080/00207144.2018.1396128

[28] He BJ, Zempel JM, Snyder AZ, Raichle ME. The temporal structures and functional significance of scale-free brain activity. Neuron. 2010;**66**(3): 353-369. DOI: 10.1016/j.neuron.2010.04.020

[29] Tukaev R. Research on the effectiveness of the universal hypnotherapy model. In: Selinski MJ, Gow KM, editors. Continuity Versus Creative Response to Challenge: The Primacy of Resilience and Resourcefulness in Life and Therapy. New York: Nova Science Publishers; 2011. pp. 499-520

[30] Tukaev RD. Universal hypnotherapy and resilience – Resourcefulness model. In: Selinski MJ, Gow KM, editors. Continuity Versus Creative Response to Challenge: The Primacy of Resilience and Resourcefulness in Life and Therapy. New York: Nova Science Publishers; 2011. pp. 451-466

[31] Raichle ME. Two views of brain function. Trends in Cognitive Sciences. 2010;**14**(4):180-190. DOI: 10.1016/j.tics.2010.01.008. PMID 20206576

[32] Raichle ME. The brain's dark energy. Scientific American. 2010;**302**(3):28-33. DOI: 10.1038/scientificamerican0310-44

[33] Yang C-C, Barrós-Loscertales A, Li M, Pinazo D, Borchardt V, Ávila C, et al. Alterations in brain structure and amplitude of low-frequency after 8 weeks of mindfulness meditation training in meditation-naïve subjects. Scientific Reports. 2019;**9**:10977. DOI: 10.1038/s41598-019-47470-4

[34] Santaella DF, Balardin JB, Afonso RF, Giorjiani GM, Sato JR, Lacerda SS, et al. Greater anteroposterior default mode network functional connectivity in long-term elderly yoga practitioners. Frontiers in Aging Neuroscience. 2019;**11**:158. DOI: 10.3389/fnagi.2019.00158

[35] Tukaev RD, Kuznetsov VE. Universal hypnotherapy and mindfulness-based therapy: Similarities, differences and therapeutic perspectives. Part 1. Society of Clinical Psychology. 2013;**23**(1):59-64 (in Russian)

[36] Tukaev RD, Kuznetsov VE. Universal hypnotherapy and mindfulness-based therapy: Similarities, differences and therapeutic perspectives. Part 2. Society of Clinical Psychology. 2013;**23**(2):67-72 (in Russian)

[37] Tukaev RD, Kuznetcov VE. Cognitive-oriented psychotherapy for anxiety disorders: Evaluation in controlled study. Society of Clinical Psychology. 2015;**25**(2):55-64 (in Russian)

[38] Tukaev RD, Zueva OP, Kuznetsov AN, Kuznetsov VV, Sryvkova KA. Complex cognitive-oriented psychotherapy of anxious disorders with panic attacks, method and results of application. Part 1. Social and Clinical Psychiatry. 2010;**20**(4): 87-93 (in Russian)

[39] Tukaev RD, Zueva OP, Kuznetsov AN, Kuznetsov VV, Sryvkova KA. Complex cognitive-oriented psychotherapy of anxious disorders with panic attacks, method and results of application. Part 2. Social and Clinical Psychiatry. 2011;**21**(2): 60-65 (in Russian)

[40] Tukaev RD. Mechanisms of psychological defense in emotional-stress psychotherapy. In: The Eighth All-Union Congress of Neuropathologists, Psychiatrists and Narcologists. Vol. 1. Moscow: Ministry of Health; 1988. pp. 506-507 (in Russian)

[41] Tukaev RD. Color induction in hypnotherapy (in system of complex emotional—stress psychotherapy of neuroses) [Doctoral dissertation]. Moscow: Moscow Research Institute of Psychiatry Ministry of Health; 1987. p. 283 (in Russian)

[42] Beresin FV. Mental and Psychophysiological Adaptation of the Person. Leningrad: Nauka Publishing; 1988 (in Russian)

[43] Khoury B, Lecomte T, Fortin G, Masse M, Therien P, Bouchard V, et al. Mindfulness-based therapy: A comprehensive meta-analysis. Clinical Psychology Review. 2013;**33**(6):763-771

[44] Demarzo MM, Montero MJ, Cuijpers P, Zabaleta-del-Olmo E, Mahtani KR, Vellinga A, et al. The efficacy of mindfulness-based interventions in primary care: A meta-analytic review. Annals of Family Medicine. 2015;**13**(6):573-582

[45] Grossenbacher PG, Quaglia JT. Contemplative cognition: A more integrative framework for advancing mindfulness and meditation research. Mindfulness. 2017;**8**:1580-1593

[46] Blanck P, Perleth S, Heidenreich T, Kroeger P, Ditzen B, Bents H, et al. Effects of mindfulness exercises as stand-alone intervention on symptoms of anxiety and depression: Systematic review and meta-analysis. Behaviour Research and Therapy. 2018;**102**:25-35

[47] Hofmann SG, Sawyer AT, Witt AA, Oh D. The effect of mindfulness-based therapy on anxiety and depression: A meta-analytic review. Journal of Consulting and Clinical Psychology. 2010;**78**(2):169-183

[48] Carmody J, Baer RA. Relationships between mindfulness practice and levels of mindfulness, medical and psychological symptoms and well-being in a mindfulness-based stress reduction program. Journal of Behavioral Medicine. 2008;**31**(1):23-33

[49] Kabat-Zinn J. An outpatient program in behavioral medicine for chronic pain patients based on the practice of mindfulness meditation: Theoretical considerations and preliminary results. General Hospital Psychiatry. 1982;**4**(1):33-47

[50] Khoury B, Sharma M, Rush SE, Fournier C. Mindfulness-based stress reduction for healthy individuals: A meta-analysis. Journal of Psychosomatic Research. 2015;**78**(6):519-528

[51] Teasdale JD, Segal Z, Williams JM. How does cognitive therapy prevent depressive relapse and why should attentional control (mindfulness) training help? Behaviour Research and Therapy. 1995;**33**(1):25-39

[52] Teasdale JD, Segal ZV, Williams JM, Ridgeway VA, Soulsby JM, Lau MA. Prevention of relapse/recurrence in major depression by mindfulness-based cognitive therapy. Journal of Consulting and Clinical Psychology. 2000;**68**(4): 615-623

[53] Evans S, Ferrando S, Findler M, Stowell C, Smart C, Haglin D. Mindfulness-based cognitive therapy for generalized anxiety disorder. Journal of Anxiety Disorders. 2008;**4**:716-721

[54] Vollestad J, Sivertsen B, Nielsen GH. Mindfulness-based stress reduction for patients with anxiety disorders: Evaluation in a randomized controlled trial. Behaviour Research and Therapy. 2011;**49**(4):281-288

[55] Tarabrina NV. Workshop on the Psychology of Post-Traumatic Stress. Saint Petersburg; 2001. p. 272 (in Russian)

[56] Spielberger CD, Gorsuch RL, Lushene RE. Manual for the State-Trait Anxiety Inventory. Palo Alto, CA: Consulting Psychologists Press; 1970

[57] Beck AT, Ward CH, Mendelson M, Mock J, Erbauch J. An inventory for measuring depression. Archives of General Psychiatry. 1961;**4**:561-571

[58] Sheehan DV. The Anxiety Disease. New York: Scribers; 1983

[59] Bohlmeijer E, ten Klooster PM, Fledderus M, Veehof M, Baer R. Psychometric properties of the five facet mindfulness questionnaire in depressed adults and development of a short form. Assessment. 2011;**18**(3):308-320

[60] Baer RA, Smith GT, Hopkins J, Krietemeyer J, Toney L. Using

self-report assessment methods to explore facets of mindfulness. Assessment. 2006;**13**(1):27-45

[61] Cohen J. Statistical Power Analysis for the Behavioral Sciences. 2nd ed. Hillsdale, NJ: Erlbaum; 1988

[62] Cumming G. Understanding the New Statistics. New York: Routledge; 2012. p. 519

Chapter 4

Inner Navigation and Theta Activity: From Movement to Cognition and Hypnosis According to the Sphere Model of Consciousness

Patrizio Paoletti, Tal Dotan Ben-Soussan and Joseph Glicksohn

Abstract

EEG theta (4–7 Hz) activity is closely related to hypnosis and hypnotic analgesia, as well as to meditation and absorption. Research further indicates that theta oscillatory power is involved in different cognitive functions, such as spatial navigation, memory, creativity, and divided attention. The current manuscript will provide a synthesis of current knowledge regarding the importance of theta's different roles in relation to hypnosis and their connections to movement. Indeed, several movement paradigms, such as Quadrato Motor Training, have been found to modulate theta activity, significantly improving cognition and emotional well-being. The utility of such movement paradigms as a therapeutic vehicle closely related to hypnosis, and the underlying characteristics allowing these neuromodulations, will be discussed. Finally, the relationships between diagonal movement and other psychological phenomena, especially intentionality, attention, and the Sphere Model of Consciousness, will be highlighted.

Keywords: hypnosis, meditation, movement, theta, EEG, Sphere Model of Consciousness

1. Introduction

Considering the many positive effects of hypnosis, such as relief from chronic pain [1, 2], the ability to enhance hypnotizability has considerable clinical utility. Hypnosis can be defined as an altered state of attention, receptivity, and concentration during which the hypnotized person is immersed in a suggestion [3–5]. Hypnosis can modulate perceptual, motor, emotional, and cognitive processes by producing changes in subjective experience and in behavior, such as greater relaxation, changes in perception of the body and/or of the environment, and increased imagination [6–8]. While neurophysiological data may not completely resolve the debate around hypnosis as an altered state of consciousness (ASC) [9, 10], they do offer interesting clues regarding the role that intentionality and specific types of attention may play in hypnosis. Furthermore, the debate about hypnosis as an ASC could benefit from a reframing in light of current theories of consciousness, particularly the Sphere Model of Consciousness (SMC).

IntechOpen

The Sphere Model of Consciousness developed by Paoletti [11–15] suggests that every experience of consciousness can be phenomenologically described as a movement within a spherical matrix. As will be illustrated in Section 4, the model provides that intentionality could be a means through which one can move from Narrative to Minimal Self and this, in turn, could allow deeper hypnotizability as well as other phenomena related to hypnosis, such as a reinterpretation of the nociceptive input underlying pain [16].

1.1 Movement and hypnosis

While different theories of hypnosis share the assumption that a hypnotic response is automatic and feels like it is happening by itself [17, 18], they do not necessarily agree on the level of intentionality and cognitive control processes that are involved. For instance, the response expectancy theory claims that expecting a behavior to happen can elicit that particular behavior; therefore, suggestions can be implemented without the involvement of intentional executive systems [19, 20]. However, expectations cannot fully account for the variance in hypnotic responding [21, 22], which is indicative of trait differences in both hypnotizability [23] and in hypnotic depth [24].

In parallel to intentionality and volition, there is a close connection between hypnosis and movement. Hypnosis may help patients to better achieve tasks of motor imagination and alter activity in the motor cortex [5]. In addition, while some argue that eye movement desensitization and reprocessing (EMDR) and hypnosis are qualitatively different, the two are often used in conjunction in therapy [25–27].

But what is the exact nature of the relationship between movement and hypnosis, and what are the possible mediating electrophysiological mechanisms between inner and outer movements and hypnosis? These are the main questions that will be addressed in this chapter. Specifically, we will discuss the possible underlying neuronal mechanisms mediating both movement and hypnosis, with a specific focus on theta activity. What we term "inner movements" and their relation to theta activity will be discussed in Section 2, focusing on hypnosis, meditation, and perceptual deprivation. This will be followed by external movement practices and their relation to such "inner movement." Consequently, we will embed our discussion within the framework of the Sphere Model of Consciousness [15] giving special attention to the Minimal Self and Narrative Self (for review see [28]). Briefly, the Minimal Self has a short temporal extension and is endowed with a sense of action, property, and first person nonconceptual content, while the Narrative Self involves personal identity and continuity through time and includes conceptual content. The SMC specifies the addition of a third state, called Overcoming of the Self, in which all sense of self disappears. Overcoming of the Self, which is parallel to consciousness without contents, has only recently been the subject of neuroscientific studies [29, 30]. It can further be compared with self-transcendence, absorption, and nondual states [31, 32].

1.2 Electrophysiological measures and hypnosis

Neural oscillations are divided into different frequency bands: both theta (4–7 Hz) and alpha (8–12 Hz) bands are associated with working memory and attention, while the gamma band (30–70 Hz) is associated with functions that include long-term memory storage and retrieval, as well as perceptual processing [33–35]. An increase in theta activity, quantified as spectral power, both frontally and globally, is a hallmark of hypnotic states [36], trance [37], meditative states [38–40], states of absorption [40], and of hypnotizability ([41]; but see [42] for an opposing view). Importantly, frontal theta activity correlates negatively with default mode network (DMN) activity [43], which is typically active during task-free resting states and is thought to represent neural processing related to mind-wandering [44, 45]. Keeping in mind that the DMN activity is automatic and is thus considered nonvoluntary, it is not surprising that electrophysiological studies based on predictive coding models[1] have focused mostly on theta activity [49, 50].

In addition, while hypnosis and hypnotizability are thought to be mediated electrophysiologically by theta activity and behaviorally by relaxation [51, 52], it is still under debate whether all hypnosis is actually autohypnosis (see for a review [53]), since motivation seems to play a central role in the process. For example, being motivated to participate in a hypnotic session and having a positive attitude about it correlates with the success of the hypnotic response and the effectiveness of the hypnotic experience [54]. This suggests that the levels of intentionality and attention could be related to the levels of hypnosis and participant susceptibility. Seemingly paradoxical, there may be a voluntary "letting go" that occurs in the hypnotic process [13, 55] related to *Overcoming of the Self*, which will be discussed further in Section 4.

At the electrophysiological level, it has been suggested that slow wave oscillations facilitate responses to suggestion, which in turn may help to explain the known variability in hypnotic responding between individuals [56]. This has been supported by findings of significantly higher levels of baseline theta activity in highly hypnotizable participants relative to those scoring "low" on hypnotizability [36, 57–61] and a tendency for hypnotic inductions to result in increases in theta activity, especially among highs [36, 62, 63].

Notably, an increase in both theta activity and alpha activity was reported among proficient meditators during meditation ([39], p. 191; [64]) and at rest ([39], p. 190), but not among those assessed for hypnotizability ([65]; note, however, that in their review, these authors only discuss the lack of a systematic relationship with alpha activity). However, the authors clarify that this increase in theta activity among proficient meditators was "the frontal midline theta generated by the anterior cingulate, dorsal, and medial prefrontal cortices" and not the "theta typically seen at the transition from Stage I to Stage II sleep...[which] originates from more widespread source" ([39], p. 202). Thus, some evidence suggests that the notion that a meditative state is essentially a hypnagogic state (the transitional state between wakefulness and sleep) or even sleep itself [66] should be replaced by the notion that a meditative state can be an intentionally prolonged hypnagogic state ([67], pp. 99–100; [68], p. 403; [69], p. 158); this, itself, would be considered to be a trance state [70]. Furthermore, as Holroyd ([71], p. 115) suggests, "a distinction is drawn between low range theta (4–6 Hz) which is associated with reverie and high range theta (5–7 Hz) which, in the frontal cortex area, is associated with loss of executive control." Mitchell, McNaughton, Flanagan, and Kirk ([72], p. 179) also suggest, "The meditation data make it possible that FM [frontal-midline]-theta is a sign that attentional resources are more internally than externally focused." Turning to change in gamma activity in the low range (25–45 Hz) in these states, there is a

[1] Predictive coding suggests that the brain generates hypotheses about the possible causes of forthcoming sensory events and that these hypotheses are compared with incoming sensory information and enables the motor system to "select appropriate responses" before an anticipated event is realized [46]. Similarly, predictive timing can be defined as the "process by which uncertainty about 'when' events are likely to occur is minimized in order to facilitate their processing and detection" [47]. At the neurophysiological level, anticipating sensory events resets the phase of delta and theta activity before the stimulus occurs [47]. Llewellyn [48] argues that REM dreaming has an elaborative role for encoding during sleep, suggesting that REM dreaming constitutes prospective coding because elaborative encoding enables inferences which, in turn, generate predictions.

decrease in frontal power [73] and an increase in posterior power [38, 73] and/or a decrease in central power [40].[2]

It is noteworthy, then, that an increase in theta activity during hypnotic induction has been found in various studies ([36, 56, 62, 63]; for review, see [78]. From [79]). Frontal theta has been found to increase with working memory load, indicating a role of theta oscillations in working memory maintenance (for review, see [43]). Theta activity increases with increasing task demands and is related to orienting, attention, memory, and affective processing mechanisms [35, 80]. Theta activity is highest at frontal midline electrodes in the resting state, indicating that the frontal theta rhythm is also detectable during rest conditions [81].

While hypnosis has been most closely linked to power in the theta band, reports suggesting changes also in gamma activity have been considered [56]. Jensen et al. [56] proposed a link between theta oscillations and hypnosis, whereby theta oscillations facilitate hypnotic responding. They further speculated that theta-gamma phase-locked oscillations may provide a physiological explanation for hypnosis by suggesting the linking of limbic and neocortical circuits [56]. However, gamma activity is known to be at possible risk of contamination from muscular activity [82] or saccade-related spike potentials (SP) due to eye movements [83].

While acknowledging that theta is associated with a large number of cognitive activities and states (including, among others, attention, orienting, decision-making, feelings of drowsiness, and emotional arousal, as noted above), it is important to emphasize that the most commonly identified roles for theta are those concerned with declarative memory coding and retrieval (for a review, see [78]) and navigation, such as maze navigation [84–86]. In parallel to navigation in the external environment, which is electrophysiologically mediated mostly by theta activity [84–86], we will suggest that:

1. Hypnosis and other "internal movement" paradigms may be regarded as mental navigation.

2. Hypnosis can be compared with external movement and navigation in space [82].

3. Internal movement paradigms, such as hypnosis and meditation, are electrophysiologically mediated, among other bands, by theta activity and require greater intentionality and attention [15].

The following section will introduce several "internal movement" techniques related to both hypnosis and meditation, as well as absorption and theta activity.

2. Inner movement

2.1 Hypnosis and absorption

Trait absorption has relevance for the study of imagery, hallucinatory or pseudo-hallucinatory experiences of altered states of consciousness, and

[2] It is noteworthy to remember that in many conditions, gamma power is phase-locked to theta activity and that both work in coordination of hippocampal networks during both waking and REM sleep [74, 75]. In addition to gamma, also beta activity is evident during both waking and REM sleep [76]. Gamma activity is further related to sensory perception, problem-solving, and memory and is thought to contribute to "binding" of sensory information (for review see [76]) and problem-solving with insight [77].

elaborate imagination [87–89]. Individuals scoring high on trait absorption will have a markedly different experiential profile compared to those scoring low on trait absorption [89, 90], and these two groups will perform differently on tasks of attentional demand [91, 92]. The overlap between high trait absorption and (1) high hypnotizability [23, 93, 94] and (2) proficiency in meditation [95] may indicate that the correlation between the two is either "significant only when both scales are administered in the same context, thus allowing the subjects to become aware that the experimenter expected to find an association between them" ([96], pp. 849–850; see also [97], but also [98], who do not find such a context effect), or the position we support that "absorbed attention may be an important prerequisite for successful long-term practice of meditation" ([69], p. 188), and that "a deeper state of absorption seems to facilitate the entrance to a deeper ASC" ([99], pp. 126–127).

The trait-state approach to hypnosis [100] suggests that the *trait* of absorption will interact with situational *context* in producing *state* absorption or a hypnotic state of consciousness. Consider what Kihlstrom ([101], p. 366) terms the "canonical design for hypnosis research," which "involves administering a standard hypnotic induction, or a control procedure, to subjects classified (on the basis of the standardized scales) as low, medium, or high in hypnotizability... Such a design permits assessments of both the correlates of hypnotizability (in the absence of hypnotic induction) and the effects of the induction procedure (independent of hypnotizability). Of particular interest, of course, is the interaction of these factors—i.e., how highly hypnotizable subjects behave following a hypnotic induction, compared to some control condition." Replace hypnotizability with absorption (the two being modestly correlated), and one can see how those scoring high on absorption behave differently from those scoring low on absorption, in much the same manner. Note further, that "Although there is acceptance that there is a general trait of hypnotic susceptibility, as measured by conventionally used standardized scales... susceptibility is also modifiable... Additionally, hypnosis in susceptibles is not a unitary state ([102], p. 62). Hence, the trait-state approach must consider a dynamic, unfolding, modifiable, interaction.

Furthermore, one can investigate concomitant electrophysiological changes in theta power in this trait-state interaction. For example, Graffin et al. [103] concluded from their study that "that the high-susceptible individuals displayed a decrease in EEG theta activity from the baseline period immediately preceding the hypnotic induction to that immediately following the induction, whereas the low-susceptible individuals showed an increase in EEG theta activity. This is consistent with the view that the high- and low-susceptible individuals are indeed in different cortical states prior to and following the hypnotic induction, that is to say, the induction procedure itself would be assumed to differentially affect high- and low-susceptible individuals." Kihlstrom ([101], p. 367) has a different take on this. He comments: "Graffin et al. interpreted the changes in theta as indicative of heightened concentration among hypnotizable subjects, but the fact that theta activity decreased in hypnotizable subjects and increased in insusceptible subjects suggests that, following the induction of hypnosis, both groups of subjects were actually in very similar cortical states." Either way, what is important here is the interaction of trait with condition in producing these shifts in theta activity.

Given that theta activity can be indicative of either the induction of a hypnagogic-like state of consciousness (which, in the present context, is closely affiliated with both meditation and hypnosis), or of highly concentrated attention [104], such shifts in theta power can be indicative of either of these. Schacter ([104], pp. 74–75) warns us that "It is not yet know whether the two "classes" of psychological events related to theta activity are essentially different processes, or whether they are different aspects of the same process ... This is a critical problem for future research. ...we might question whether it is plausible to accept that theta activity observed during zazen concentration in experienced meditators indexes psychological processes that are similar to those observed in college-age volunteers when concentrating on a mental arithmetic problem." Thus, even though, as White, et al. ([105], p. 98) have noted, the "correlation between baseline theta and hypnotizability has been described as a robust finding in the literature, proposed to result from attentional differences between high and low susceptibility groups," without a close analysis of how such theta activity is related to the actual performance of those scoring low or high on absorption, we will remain with the problem underlined by Schacter [104]. What is promising is that "findings showing differences between highs and lows in both the *patterns* of associations between EEG-assessed bandwidth activity and subjects' phenomenological experience of hypnosis ... and in the brain *areas* (source locations) associated with theta and beta activity...." ([56], p. 44).

Speaking of beta, it was further found that the hypnotic depth and increased imagery and exceptionality of the hypnotic experience in highly suggestible individuals were related to fast frequencies, including beta and gamma, while the lows exhibited negative correlations between imagery on the one hand and theta and beta on the other [106].

In this context, it should also be kept in mind that beta oscillatory activity is likely to have a functional role in response selection, resembling attentional modulation of alpha activity [107]. Beta modulation was found also following "animal hypnosis," also known as "tonic immobility" or "immobility reflex".

The modulation depended on type of induction and session number [108, 109], supporting previous evidence that beta power has also been implicated in broader cognitive processes [107] in addition to movement and response inhibition [107].

2.2 Meditation

Meditators have been found to score higher on trait absorption than controls [95, 110]. In addition, increased theta and alpha power, reflecting activity of multifunctional neuronal networks and differentially associated with orienting, attention, memory, affective, and cognitive processing, is evident in meditators [80]. Altered theta and alpha activity has consistently been reported following meditation [111]. In fact, numerous studies conducted with Western meditators, usually having less than 10 years' experience, have reported increased power and coherence in the alpha and theta frequency bands during meditation practice [39, 111, 112]. Increased gamma power has also been reported in studies with advanced meditative practitioners [38, 73, 113, 114].

Consistent with previous meditation research (for review see [115]), also Berman and Stevens [116] found increased delta (0–4 Hz), theta, and alpha activity during meditation. When differentiating between general meditation and nondual states (in which the participant transcends the separation between self and other), the opposite trend was observed for gamma, which was higher during the meditation sessions in entirely compared to the nondual state [116]. Similarly, Berkovich-Ohana et al. [73], who examined three levels of mindfulness expertise and controls, found that mindfulness practitioners generally exhibited reduced resting-state frontal low gamma power as compared to controls, as well as decreased resting-state gamma functional connectivity representing DMN deactivation in the long-term practitioners, suggesting a trait/long-lasting effect of reduced mind-wandering and self-related processing [73, 117]. In addition, creativity, as measured by ideational fluency and flexibility, which were higher in the long-term practitioners than short-term practitioners and control participants, was negatively correlated with gamma interhemispheric functional connectivity [118]. Thus, one should keep in mind that different mediation techniques can produce different electrophysiological results, depending among others on the depth of the experience and the experimental design [116].

2.3 OVO Whole-Body Perceptual Deprivation (OVO-WBPD)

As we will see in the current section, studies examining perceptual movement, where movement is absent and stillness is the main feature, were also found to be related mostly on delta waves. While delta has historically been associated with sleep and pathological processes, it has recently been found to be related to both autonomic and metabolic processes, suggesting that it is involved in integration of cerebral activity with homeostatic processes, as well as in motivation and reward, as delta also increases during hunger, sexual arousal, and sustained pain [119]. Delta activity is further related to attention, salience detection, and subliminal perception, consistent with meditative states and absorption [116, 119, 120], such as in the case of Yoga Nidra [121][3].

In-line with previous research linking delta waves in meditative states [125], a recent study examined the effects of the OVO Whole-Body Perceptual Deprivation (OVO-WBPD) chamber effects on absorption in experienced meditators. The OVO, an altered sensory environment, is in the form of a human-sized egg ("uovo" means egg in Italian), within which the subject cannot easily perceive spatial coordinates. Based on the Sphere Model of Consciousness, the OVO-WBPD was specifically built with the aim of facilitating an immersive experience and an increased state of *presence* [11]. Ben-Soussan et al. [120], who studied participants who were instructed to "rest as best as they can" in the OVO chamber, found an increased state of absorption, which was accompanied by enhanced delta and lower theta activity, as well as beta (13–20 Hz) activity, peaking in the insula. These results may suggest an enhanced effort to sensory-integrate interoceptive signals.

In addition to the insula [120], theta was further linked to another main area of the salience network, namely, the anterior cingulate [126–131]. While DMN activity is negatively correlated with both hypnosis and theta activity [129–131], the salience network is thought to support the detection of subjectively important events and the mobilization of attentional and working memory resources in the service of goal-directed behavior [132–134].

[3] Yoga Nidra is defined as a "state in which an individual demonstrates all the symptoms of deep, non-REM sleep, including delta brain waves, while simultaneously remaining fully conscious [121]. In addition, it is important to note that while meditation spindles have similar amplitudes to those in sleep, all other parameters are significantly different, with more-experienced subjects displaying high-voltage slow waves reminiscent, but significantly different, to the slow waves of deeper stages of non-REM sleep [122]. In addition, they also differ from slow delta activity in anesthesia which is notably less rhythmic and coherent [122]. Most importantly, the main regions of interest are notably different to those in sleep [122, 123]. More specifically, the significant presence of limbic sources in meditation support the hypothesis of the effects of meditation on memory and spatial and temporal orientation, and consequently to the ventral and dorsal streams of attention and feeling- and salience-based, respectively [122]. The electrophysiological change induced by these type of training, together with the ability to remain consciously aware while producing delta waves, is believed to be associated with attaining a highly stabilized state of higher consciousness [121, 124] and the integration of transcendental experiences in both waking, dreaming, and sleeping [125].

As in the case of perceptual deprivation, different meditative states have also been found to be related to decreased DMN activity [73, 135–137]. Similarly, hypnosis was found to be related to decreased DMN activity [138] and suspending habitual modes of attention and achieving refined states of meta-awareness [139]. In fact, hypnotic induction increased subjective ratings of attentional absorption and decreased ratings of mind-wandering. Moreover, these changes were associated with decreased DMN activity and increased activity in prefrontal attention networks [138].

3. External movement

As indicated above, according to Jensen et al. [78], hypnosis can be viewed as a use of suggestions for creating changes in thoughts, feelings, or behaviors when the clinician views the client as having enough theta power to be able to respond to those suggestions. Jensen indicates that "hypnotic strategies, then, could include (1) *any* strategy that enhances slow oscillations (using traditional hypnotic inductions, but also any technique that has been or is ultimately shown to increase slow oscillations) and/or being aware of behavioral signs indicating an increase in or adequate level of theta, coupled with (2) suggestions that enhance existing connections among neuron assemblies (e.g., those consistent with the subject experiencing of himself or herself with useful images or having a positive view of the future) or that create new ones" ([78], p. 15). It is, therefore, relevant to note that there is an increase in theta activity and a corresponding increase in either alpha activity or a global increase in spectral power (including within the alpha and theta bands) during exercise [140, 141]. Fascinatingly, there is even evidence of a higher degree of both alpha and theta activity during eyes-closed restful wakefulness in proficient athletes [142].

These converging lines of thought together with Dietrich [143, 144] support the connection between hypnosis, meditation, and acute exercise, which all result in prefrontal hypoactivation. Consequently, we now address the presence of increased theta activity following specifically structured bodily movement, focusing on several specific examples involving different degrees of diagonal movement.

3.1 Diagonal movement

It has been suggested that rhythmical bilateral diagonal body movement improves motor and cognitive functions [145, 146], such as creativity and cognitive flexibility, similar to findings for hypnosis/mediation. However, no study that we are aware of has actually examined electrophysiological changes during diagonal body movements. The diagonal axis has the role of a metaphorical rule-breaker in relation to *the way of thinking*, as suggested by the definition of "diagonal thinking" as a mixture of logical (i.e., vertical) and creative (i.e., lateral) thinking [147]. Diagonal movements are widely used in disciplines based on whole-body movements such as tai chi, and recent paradigms such as Quadrato Motor Training, which will be discussed below.

Shapiro [148, 149], in her original description of EMDR, proposed that its directed eye movements mimic the saccades of rapid eye movement sleep (REM), known to be electrophysiologically related to synchronous theta waves [75, 150]. In addition, Stickgold [151, 152] proposed that the repetitive redirecting of attention during EMDR induces a neurobiological state similar to that of REM sleep. Additional study findings have supported the hypothesis that EMDR promotes the transfer of episodic memory to semantic memory, which will then be consolidated during REM-like (4–6 Hz) states [153][4,5].

As mentioned above, activation of frontal areas and especially the anterior cingulate that occurs during hypnosis matches well with the behavioral changes occurring in hypnotic state, such as the intensification of focused attention (for review see [159]). Importantly, the anterior cingulate has known anatomical connections with the frontal eye field and supplementary eye field and thus plays a prominent role in regulating eye movements, such as maintenance of visual fixation and suppression of reflexive saccades [159]. For example, classical behavioral marker of hypnosis, namely, the *hypnotically induced stare*, is a glazed look in the eyes accompanied by a highly reduced eye blinking rate and inimitable changes in the patterns of eye movements and pupil size [159]. Pupil size was recently found to be closely related to a variety of cognitive processes, such as decision-making [160]. In turn positive correlations were only found in the high-gamma band (60–100 Hz) and were similar in both wake and sleep conditions.

Only a few recent studies have examined electrophysiological changes during diagonal movements. A rare pioneering study [161] has found increased frontal theta activity during the initiation of diagonal movement, compared to purely vertical movements, which were also studied. The increased frontal theta was possibly due to greater computational effort [86, 95, 140]. Source localization further showed that the increased frontal theta activity was generated in the middle frontal cortex. In addition, the authors found a biphasic pattern of frontoparietal alpha/beta modulations during vertical movements.

Rimbert et al. [5] reported modulation in sensorimotor beta and theta activity during real movement and motor imagery; Marson et al. [161] also found biphasic modulation of alpha activity related to the second part of vertical movements (*each movement was composed of two parts, a forward and comeback period, the biphasic response in the comeback period during vertical movement).* More specifically, the decreased alpha activity was observed immediately after the start of the comeback period, and, consequently, there was an increase in the same frequency band tied to the end of the movement. The decreased alpha activity observed immediately after the end of the second movement could reflect a decrease in internalized attention, as decreased alpha activity is classically related to decreased focus on internal states and amplified processing of environmental information through sensorial inputs,

---

4 More specifically, as Pagani et al. [154] detail, delta activity is related to slow wave sleep, which in turn is related to transferring edited memories from the hippocampus to the neocortex, as well as to stimulating the integration of these into neocortical neuronal networks, while theta activity is related to REM sleep. Bilateral stimulation typical of EMDR causes immediate slowing of the depolarization rate of neurons from the dominant waking state frequency of around 7 Hz to about 1.5 Hz. Interestingly, as Pagani [154] further noted, animal research has demonstrated that low-frequency (5 Hz) stimulation can cause a depotentiation of amygdala AMPA receptors involved in the retention of traumatic memory and 900 stimuli at 1–5 Hz depotentiated synapses mediating memory, suggesting that memories aroused during therapy are reactivated, replayed, and encoded into existing memory networks. Interestingly, delta activity occurs as waves during bilateral stimulation in other frequency waves (such as beta) and is related to eye movements. Lastly, Pagani et al. [154] suggested that the consolidation of emotional memory in the neocortex during an EMDR session, which often results in a sudden symptoms disappearance, is associated with periods in which slow (1.5 Hz) and faster (theta-alpha) activity are elicited by the alternation of bilateral stimulation and improved cognition.

5 Similarly to EMDR, also binaural beat, which requires bilateral stimulation, by presenting two slightly different wave forms to each ear via stereophonic headphones, thus generating a third "beat" frequency, was found to be related to hypnotic susceptibility and theta activity ([154–156], yet see [42]), suggesting in turn also complex dynamic interactions between the two hemispheres [157]. For example, beat frequencies in theta and alpha range both increased interhemispheric coherence selectively at alpha frequencies [158].

especially the visual system [159, 160]. Similar to Rimbert et al. [5], Marson et al. [161] further found post-movement beta rebound [162] between consecutive trials, namely, increased beta activity both in diagonal and vertical movements.

3.2 Quadrato Motor Training (QMT)

Quadrato Motor Training is a mindful movement practice based on the Sphere Model of Consciousness. Participants are asked to move within a square (*quadrato*, in Italian), according to a specific sequence of instructions. QMT requires a high level of attention divided between the body and the spatial coordinates incorporated in the quadrato space, as well as silent waiting for the next instruction. Previous studies showed that QMT enhances theta activity and improves cognition (for a recent review, see [163, 164]). At the behavioral level, these changes have been associated with improvements in cognitive and psycho-emotional functioning [162, 165–167], considered important aspects of health and well-being.

What appears to make QMT different from other forms of physical activity is its impact on interhemispheric functional connectivity in the theta and alpha bands. In contrast to studies of other types of physical activity that focused on local changes in activity and have usually not reported changes in long-range connectivity, studies of healthy populations engaging in QMT have demonstrated both increased EEG power [168, 169] and coherence [170–173], especially in the theta and alpha bands. Indeed, both single sessions and protracted periods of QMT were found to result in increased intra- and interhemispheric functional connectivity in the theta and alpha bands [170–173]. Increased theta and alpha functional connectivity is thought to reflect improved cognitive functions and higher states of consciousness, due to better integration of information and communication across brain regions [174–176]. As such, these findings provide additional evidence relating to QMT's capacity to promote cognitive and psycho-emotional well-being.

Moreover, Ben-Soussan et al. [170] also found improved spatial cognition and reflectivity in groups who underwent a single session of QMT, in comparison to two control groups that underwent either simple motor or verbal training. The improvements were thought to stem from changes in functional connectivity, as evidenced by changes in intra- and interhemispheric coherence in theta and alpha bands [170].

Until recently, there has been a paucity of studies that investigated neural modulation during meditative movement. In a recent pilot study, De Fano et al. [163] examined five volunteers performing a single session of QMT characterized by three "blocks" which are rounds of the QMT routine. Since QMT requires executive control, which involves frontal theta activity, higher frontal theta power toward the last of the three QMT blocks, compared to the starting one, is expected. Indeed, a trend of increased theta activity was observed toward the last two blocks compared to the first one, which may reflect not only the cognitive control required by QMT performance but also the increase in cognitive effort that occurs overtime [163].

Going back to the theme of navigation and its connection to attention and salience dorsal and ventral streams discussed above, which are further related to the superior and inferior longitudinal fasciculi [177], 6 weeks of daily QMT was further found to increase white matter integrity as indicated by increased fractional anisotropy in the superior and inferior longitudinal fasciculi, as well as in additional tracts related to sensorimotor and cognitive functions [165].

3.3 Tai chi and qigong

Another meditative movement paradigm, tai chi, has been more heavily studied. Several electroencephalography EEG studies have reported that tai chi can produce changes in mental state or electroencephalogram patterns associated with other alterations of cognitive or physical indices. An early study by Pan et al. [178] examined the difference in EEG theta between concentrative and non-concentrative qigong states, demonstrating that the frontal midline theta rhythm was related to the concentrative qigong state. As the theta rhythm has been suggested as one of the normal EEG patterns occurring in mental concentration, the authors concluded that the theta rhythm is an indicator of mental concentration during qigong. Notably, Field et al. [179] observed that performance on math computations significantly improved after a 20-min tai chi/ yoga training course and was associated with increased frontal theta activity. Field et al. [179] further found a trend of increased theta activity and decreased self-reported anxiety, and the authors attributed this to the relaxation effects of tai chi. This increased frontal theta activity was replicated in a study of skilled female tai chi practitioners, showing a pattern typically occurring during states of relaxation and attention [180].

Additional support for the importance of external movement, in parallel to inner movement and their possible connection, related to theta activity, comes from the fact that frequent movement is preferable to one's health over sedentary behavior, making movement therapies, when applied correctly, beneficial to chronic pain conditions, by ameliorating pain and related symptoms [181]. Moreover, the reported benefits are not only strictly related to musculoskeletal or vascular function but also with the mental dimension of well-being. For example, mindful movement practices, such as tai chi, have been found to significantly help in chronic pain management, for conditions such as osteoarthritis, low back pain, and fibromyalgia (for review, see [182]).

4. The Sphere Model of Consciousness and the position within the sphere

The Sphere Model of Consciousness [15] aims to symbolize the phenomenology of consciousness utilizing the geometrical properties of spatial coordinates within a spherical framework (see **Figure 1**).

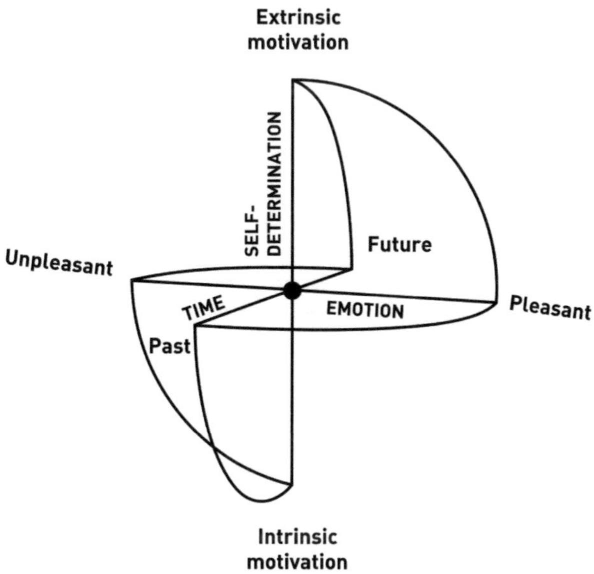

Figure 1.
The Sphere Model of Consciousness (adapted from [11, 13, 15]).

Each axis of the SMC represents the deployment and polarity of an aspect of experience, with an equilibrium point in the center of the sphere and a graduated scale indicating distance from the center. The center of the sphere represents an equilibrium point, with respect to three spatial coordinates, namely: (1) a horizontal *emotion axis* (e.g., representing the emotional polarities of unpleasant and pleasant), (2) a vertical *self-determination axis* representing the dimensions of value and aspiration [15], and (3) a *time axis* (e.g., representing the temporal deployment of past to future). The center can be considered a state of "Overcoming the Self," that is, a state of neutrality and detachment from the usual experiences of the Narrative and Minimal selves [15], which is crucial to hypnosis and different meditative practices [183]. Berkovich-Ohana and Glicksohn [28] suggested that experiences related to the Narrative Self are perceived as further away from the body, more abstract, and related to the future and the past. Narrative Self, Minimal Self, and Overcoming of the Self are represented in the SMC as concentric circles around the center of the sphere, with greater distance from the center signifying a more abstract experience of oneself. We shall now merge the electrophysiological and neuroanatomical findings in order to see how one can voluntarily move toward the center of the sphere.

5. The importance of attention and intentionally moving toward the center of the sphere

Movement, volition, and cognition are deeply related [188, 189] and, as seen above, are all related to theta activity. In fact, it has been suggested that the nervous system has evolved to allow active movement and provide a goal-oriented plan; as such, motivation and emotion represent facets of a common phenomenon. That commonality is the motivational-emotional system, which interacts with learning and higher-order cognition [184, 185]. In contrast to meditation practices, which are thought to involve and cultivate mindfulness (being aware of one's current mental state; about the problems in defining mindfulness, see [186, 187]), different theories of hypnosis posit that the hypnotic response is a form of strategic self-deception in regard to one's mental state [188]. Thus, it has been suggested that hypnotic response implies a lack of mindfulness, at least regarding particular mental states about which one is strategically deceived [188].

However, we suggest that it is also the combination of attention and intentionality (and not self-deception), which should be addressed in regard to hypnosis and other states of mind [13–15]. People often engage in meditation training because they believe it will result in a specific positive outcome, having received suggestions regarding its potential benefits [56]. Such suggestions—here in the form of self-suggestions, also known as outcome expectancies—are in-line with social cognitive views of hypnosis [10, 189] that posit that hypnosis can be viewed as a use of suggestions for creating changes in thoughts, feelings, or behaviors [56]. As such, self-suggestion implies both attention and intentionality.

Importantly, as noted earlier, frontal theta EEG activity correlates negatively with default mode network activity [43]. Recalling that high theta activity facilitates response to suggestions (e.g., [56]) and plays an important role in attention [80] and intention, such as intentional learning, and intentional movement [190, 191], we suggest that the combination of attention and intention may help to explain the known variability in hypnotic responding between individuals. This, in turn, suggests that the level of hypnotizability can be related to the participant's baseline position within the sphere [14, 15]. Together, these may have significant implications for the success of treatments.

Numerous studies have highlighted the importance of hypnosis in various clinical conditions, such as chronic pain [192]. Pain is a conscious experience, which can be considered an interpretation of the nociceptive input and potentially influenced by many factors, such as memories, emotions, and cognitions [16]. Decreased temporal-parietal theta (as well as alpha) activity during pain is consistent with a pain-related activation of the insula [193], which is known to be involved in pain processes [16]. Decreased theta connectivity was also found between the insula and the DMN in fibromyalgia, which may reflect persistent pain encoding associated with the chronic pain state in the disorder [194]. Maladaptive rumination and the re-experience of symptoms, which occur in many chronic pain conditions [195], and are known to be related to the DMN [196–198], were further found to be related to decreased theta band networks in post trauma [199]. Thus, finding ways to voluntarily move from the maladaptive and automatic narrative, which is predominant in these conditions, may aid in ameliorating symptoms.

In fact, studies found decreased DMN activation following hypnosis [138]. Decreased DMN activation, following different therapeutic approaches, is further linked to improvements in pain-related catastrophizing, which is generally self-referential, negative, and automatic [200]. In addition, there is growing evidence that mindfulness, as a volitionally initiated cognitive act, can significantly attenuate the subjective experience of pain [201]. Thus, cultivating experiential openness and acceptance, anchored in the embodied minimal self, and not in the narrative/default self, can reduce pain unpleasantness and lead to a reduction of symptoms in chronic pain patients [202, 203].

Emphasizing the importance of intentionality and its electrophysiological markers can further aid in differentiating hypnosis from "animal hypnosis" or "tonic immobility." "Animal hypnosis" has been found to effect electrophysiological state, such as altering beta, gamma, and alpha activities, depending on the method of induction, duration, and number of sessions [108, 109]. Nevertheless, one should keep in mind that while "animal hypnosis" can be induced in different ways, ranging from restraint to visual fixation, they are all involuntary [204], while the degrees of freedom in human hypnosis, although debatable, are greater. In fact, "tonic immobility" is physiologically quite different in physiological terms (i.e., defense and anti-predation reactions) [8, 205] and is controlled by a motor inhibitory system [204]. Thus, it is not surprising that in contrast to hypnosis, tonic immobility is more related to decreased theta activity and increased delta activity [108, 109], which are both inversely related to intentionality and volition [206]. Together these emphasize the importance of the intentionality aspect in human hypnosis. Nevertheless, it has been argued that hypnotic ability in humans may have evolved at least in part to allow for the control of pain and anxiety after injury, thereby reducing the likelihood of attack by predators [207].

In conclusion, although not a systematic review of this topic, this chapter offers three primary ideas for further consideration: (1) hypnosis and other "internal movement" paradigms may be regarded as mental navigation, (2) they can be compared to external movement and navigation in space, and (3) they are electrophysiologically mediated primarily by theta activity and require greater intentionality and attention. Based on the SMC, this may be related to an intentional shift away from DMN activity, which is anticorrelated with theta activity, and toward clear goal direction, represented by the center of the sphere. Thus, combined multidisciplinary examination of the connection between consciousness and hypnosis, encompassing cognitive psychology and motor and contemplative neuroscience, would produce greater theoretical understanding and implications on consciousness and hypnosis practice. First, in order to reach our personal and social aims, one can and should train to internally move intentionally from an automatic Narrative to the Minimal self, and eventually reach the state of Overcoming the Self, in order to know and better master one's own perceptions and mental processing. This idea is also related to the works of Charles Tart [208], who describes our ordinary everyday experience as being in a state similar to hypnotic trance, where we are not sleeping but neither are we truly awake. The solution to this state of affairs, similarly to current contemplative neuroscience results presented here, necessitates waking up to our true selves through a process of self-observation and self-remembrance [11, 12, 14, 208].

Second, the parallels between these two lines of research, namely, the similar electrophysiological modulation present in hypnosis, real movement, and motor imagery and the findings related to diagonal movement, can have a useful impact on the field; it can do so by helping to validate reliable electrophysiological effects of hypnosis and increase our understanding of the related biological mechanisms and connections to internal and external movement. If confirmed in future research, these ideas may have important implications for enhancing the response to hypnosis treatments and for customized, combined therapeutic modalities. In turn, emphasizing the importance of intentional inner and outer navigation and their electrophysiological signature can also aid in differentiating between the different techniques and their possible synergetic effects.

In summary, as we know, hypnosis has many benefits, including the relief of chronic pain. These benefits are possible due to knowledge gained related to how the mind works and thus the possibility of leading it into specific mental and neural states, as is the case with hypnosis. The investigation of the connections between hypnosis and theta activity, among others, further demonstrates an affinity between meditative practices and hypnosis, and that intentionality can play an important role in leading oneself into desired states. In these states we are able to know ourselves better and master our perceptions and the interpretation we give of them. Training ourselves in this direction can, therefore, improve our well-being and quality of life. Future studies should combine behavioral, neuroanatomical, and electrophysiological measures to help in distinguishing different types of hypnotic states and practices, as well as to examine the role of the person's detached and attentive intentionality in reaching them.

Author details

Patrizio Paoletti[1], Tal Dotan Ben-Soussan[1*] and Joseph Glicksohn[2,3]

1 Research Institute for Neuroscience, Education and Didactics, Fondazione Patrizio Paoletti, Assisi, Italy

2 Department of Criminology, Bar-Ilan University, Israel

3 The Leslie and Susan Gonda (Goldschmied) Multidisciplinary Brain Research Center, Bar-Ilan University, Israel

*Address all correspondence to: research@fondazionepatriziopaoletti.org

References

[1] De Benedittis G. Hypnosis and biofeedback for the control of chronic pain. In: Mocavero G, Gullo A, Paladini VA, Romano E, editors. Recent Advances in Anaesthesia Pain Intensive Care and Emergency. Trieste: A.P.I.C.E. Ed; 1989. pp. 119-131

[2] Liossi C, Popi H. Clinical hypnosis versus cognitive behavioral training for pain management with pediatric cancer patients undergoing bone marrow aspirations. The International Journal of Clinical and Experimental Hypnosis. 1999;**47**(2):104-116

[3] Erickson M. Hypnosis in painful terminal illness. The American Journal of Clinical Hypnosis. 1958;**56**:67-71

[4] Malrewicz JA, Godin J, Milton H. Erickson: de l'Hypnose Clinique à la Psychothérapie Stratégique. Paris: ESF Ed.; 1986. p. 156

[5] Rimbert S et al. Hypnotic state modulates sensorimotor beta rhythms during real movement and motor imagery. Frontiers in Psychology. 2019;**10**:2341

[6] Spiegel H, Spiegel D. Trance and Treatment: Clinical Uses of Hypnosis. 2nd rev. Washington DC: American Psychiatric Pub; 2008. p. 576

[7] Rainville P, Hofbauer RK, Bushnell MC, Duncan GH, Price DD. Hypnosis modulates activity in brain structures involved in the regulation of consciousness. Cognitive Neuroscience. 2002;**14**(6):887-901

[8] Oakley DA, Halligan PW. Hypnotic suggestion: Opportunities for cognitive neuroscience. Nature Reviews Neuroscience. 2013;**14**(8):565-576

[9] Lynn S et al. Mindfulness, acceptance, and hypnosis: Cognitive and clinical perspectives. The International Journal of Clinical and Experimental Hypnosis. 2006;**54**(2):143-166

[10] Lynn S, Kirsch IR, Hallquist MN. Social cognitive theories of hypnosis. In: Nash JA, Barnier A, editors. The Oxford Handbook of Hypnosis: Theory, Research, and Practice. Oxford, UK: Oxford University Press; 2008. pp. 111-139

[11] Paoletti P. Flussi, Territori, Luogo [Flows, Territories, Place]. Madeira, Portugal: M.E.D. Publishing; 2002

[12] Paoletti P. Flussi, Territori, Luogo II [Flows, Territories, Place II]. Madeira, Portugal: M.E.D. Publishing; 2002

[13] Paoletti P. Crescere nell'eccellenza. Rome, Italy: Armando Publishing; 2008. p. 176

[14] Paoletti P, Selvaggio A. Osservazione. Perugia, Italy: Edizioni 3P; 2011. p. 120

[15] Paoletti P, Ben Soussan TD. The Sphere Model of Consciousness: From geometrical to neuro-psycho-educational perspectives. Logica Universalis. 2019;**13**(3):395-415

[16] Mordeniz C. Pain perception within consciousness. NeuroQuantology. 2016;**14**(2):439-446

[17] Godot D. Formulating hypnotic suggestions. In: Handbook of Medical and Psychological Hypnosis: Foundations, Applications, and Professional Issues. New York: Springer Publishing Company; 2016. p. 57

[18] Spanos NP. Hypnotic behavior: A social-psychological interpretation of amnesia, analgesia and "trance logic". Behavioral and Brain Sciences. 1986;**9**(3):449-467. DOI: 10.1017/S0140525X00046537

[19] Kirsch I. Response expectancy as a determinant of experience and

behavior. The American Psychologist. 1985;**40**(11):1189

[20] Kirsch I. Response expectancy theory and application: A decennial review. Applied and Preventive Psychology. 1997;**6**(2):69-79

[21] Benham G et al. Expect the unexpected: Ability, attitude, and responsiveness to hypnosis. Journal of Personality and Social Psychology. 2006;**91**(2):342

[22] Shor RE et al. Relation of predicted to actual hypnotic responsiveness, with special reference to posthypnotic amnesia. The International Journal of Clinical and Experimental Hypnosis. 1984;**32**(4):376-387

[23] Glisky ML, Tataryn DJ, Tobias BA, Kihlstrom JF, McConkey KM. Absorption, openness to experience, and hypnotizability. Journal of Personality and Social Psychology. 1991;**60**(2):263-272. DOI: 10.1037/0022-3514.1060.1032.1263

[24] Tellegen A, Atkinson G. Openness to absorbing and self-altering experiences ("absorption"), a trait related to hypnotic susceptibility. Journal of Abnormal Psychology. 1974;**83**(3):268-277. DOI: 10.1037/h0036681

[25] Hollander HE, Bender SS. ECEM (eye closure eye movements): Integrating aspects of EMDR with hypnosis for treatment of trauma. The American Journal of Clinical Hypnosis. 2001;**43**(3-4):187-202

[26] Beere DB, Simon MJ, Welch K. Recommendations and illustrations for combining hypnosis and EMDR in the treatment of psychological trauma. The American Journal of Clinical Hypnosis. 2001;**43**(3-4):217-231

[27] Fine CG, Berkowitz AS. The wreathing protocol: The imbrication of hypnosis and EMDR in the treatment of dissociative identity disorder and other dissociative responses. The American Journal of Clinical Hypnosis. 2001;**43**(3-4):275-290

[28] Berkovich-Ohana A, Glicksohn J. The consciousness state space (CSS)—A unifying model for consciousness and self. Frontiers in Psychology. 2014;**5**:341

[29] Hinterberger T et al. Decreased electrophysiological activity represents the conscious state of emptiness in meditation. Frontiers in Psychology. 2014;**5**:99

[30] Winter U et al. Content-free awareness: EEG-fcMRI correlates of consciousness as such in an expert meditator. Frontiers in Psychology. 2019;**10**:3.064-3.074

[31] Josipovic Z. Neural correlates of nondual awareness in meditation. Annals of the New York Academy of Sciences. 2014;**1307**(1):9-18

[32] Vieten C et al. Future directions in meditation research: Recommendations for expanding the field of contemplative science. PLoS One. 2018;**13**(11):1-30

[33] Başar-Eroğlu C, Başar E, Demiralp T, Schürmann M. P300-response: Possible psychophysiological correlates in delta and theta frequency channels. A review. International Journal of Psychophysiology. 1992;**13**:161-179

[34] Başar E, Başar-Eroğlu C, Karakaş S, Schürmann M. Are cognitive processes manifested in event-related gamma, alpha, theta and delta oscillations in the EEG? Neuroscience Letters. 1999;**259**:165-168

[35] Başar E, Başar-Eroğlu C, Karakaş S, Schürmann M. Gamma, alpha, delta, and theta oscillations govern cognitive processes. International Journal of Psychophysiology. 2001;**39**:241-248

[36] Sabourin ME, Cutcomb SD, Crawford HJ, Pribram K. EEG correlates of hypnotic susceptibility and hypnotic trance: Spectral analysis and coherence. International Journal of Psychophysiology. 1990;**10**(2):125-142. DOI: 10.1016/0167-8760(1090)90027-B

[37] Oohashi T, Kawai N, Honda M, Nakamura S, Morimoto M, Nishina E, et al. Electroencephalographic measurement of possession trance in the field. Clinical Neurophysiology. 2002;**113**(3):435-445

[38] Cahn BR, Delorme A, Polich J. Occipital gamma activation during Vipassana meditation. Cognitive Processing. 2010;**11**(1):39-56. DOI: 10.1007/s10339-10009-10352-10331

[39] Cahn BR, Polich J. Meditation states and traits: EEG, ERP, and neuroimaging studies. Psychological Bulletin. 2006;**132**(2):180-211. DOI: 10.1037/0033-2909.1132.1032.1180

[40] DeLosAngeles D, Williams G, Burston J, Fitzgibbon SP, Lewis TW, Grummett TS, et al. Electroencephalographic correlates of states of concentrative meditation. International Journal of Psychophysiology. 2016;**110**:27-39

[41] Ray WJ. EEG concomitants of hypnotic susceptibility. International Journal of Clinical and Experimental Hypnosis. 1997;**45**(3):301-313. DOI: 10.1080/00207149708416131

[42] Stevens L, Haga Z, Queen B, Brady B, Adams D, Gilbert J, et al. Binaural beat induced theta EEG activity and hypnotic susceptibility: Contradictory results and technical considerations. The American Journal of Clinical Hypnosis. 2003;**45**(4):295-309

[43] Scheeringa R, Bastiaansen MC, Petersson KM, Oostenveld R, Norris DG, Hagoort P. Frontal theta EEG activity correlates negatively with the default mode network in resting state. International Journal of Psychophysiology. 2008;**67**(3):242-251

[44] Buckner RL, Andrews-Hanna JR, Schacter DL. The brain's default network: Anatomy, function, and relevance to disease. In: Kingstone A, Miller MB, editors. The Year in Cognitive Neuroscience. Malden, MA: Blackwell; 2008. pp. 1-38

[45] Raichle ME, MacLeod AM, Snyder AZ, Powers WJ, Gusnard DA, Shulman GL. A default mode of brain function. Proceedings of the National Academy of Sciences of the United States of America. 2001;**98**:676-682. DOI: 10.1073/pnas.98.2.676

[46] Schütz-Bosbach S, Prinz W. Prospective coding in event representation. Cognitive Processing. 2007;**8**(2):93-102

[47] Friston K, Kiebel S. Predictive coding under the free-energy principle. Philosophical Transactions of the Royal Society, B: Biological Sciences. 2009;**364**(1521):1211-1221

[48] Llewellyn S. Dream to predict? REM dreaming as prospective coding. Frontiers in Psychology. 2016;**6**:1961

[49] Mehta MR. Neuronal dynamics of predictive coding. The Neuroscientist. 2001;7(6):490-495. DOI: 10.1177/107385840100700605

[50] Friston K, Mattout J, Kilner J. Action understanding and active inference. Biological Cybernetics. 2011;**104**(1-2):137-160. DOI: 10.1007/s00422-011-0424-z

[51] Batty MJ, Bonnington S, Tang BK, Hawken MB, Gruzelier JH. Relaxation strategies and enhancement of hypnotic susceptibility: EEG neurofeedback, progressive muscle relaxation and self-hypnosis. Brain Research Bulletin. 2006;**71**(1-3):83-90

[52] Jensen MP, Hakimian S, Sherlin LH, Fregni F. New insights into neuromodulatory approaches for the treatment of pain. The Journal of Pain. 2008;**9**(3):193-199

[53] Zeig JK. An Ericksonian approach to hypnosis: The phenomenological model of hypnosis; the nature of hypnotic "states"; multilevel communication and indirection; and why all hypnosis is not self-hypnosis. Australian Journal of Clinical & Experimental Hypnosis. 2008;**36**(2):99-114

[54] Spanos NP, Barber TX. Toward a convergence in hypnosis research. The American Psychologist. 1974;**29**(7):500-511

[55] Brown KW, Leary MR, editors. The Oxford Handbook of Hypo-egoic Phenomena. Oxford: Oxford University Press; 2016

[56] Jensen MP, Adachi T, Hakimian S. Brain oscillations, hypnosis, and hypnotizability. The American Journal of Clinical Hypnosis. 2015;**57**(3): 230-253

[57] Freeman R, Barabasz A, Barabasz M, Warner D. Hypnosis and distraction differ in their effects on cold pressor pain. The American Journal of Clinical Hypnosis. 2000;**43**(2):137-148

[58] Galbraith GC, London P, Leibovitz MP, Cooper LM, Hart JT. EEG and hypnotic susceptibility. Journal of Comparative and Physiological Psychology. 1970;**72**(1):125-131

[59] Kirenskaya AV, Novototsky-Vlasov VY, Zvonikov VM. Waking EEG spectral power and coherence differences between high and low hypnotizable subjects. The International Journal of Clinical and Experimental Hypnosis. 2011;**59**(4):441-453

[60] Montgomery DD, Dwyer KV, Kelly SM. Relationship between QEEG relative power and hypnotic susceptibility. The American Journal of Clinical Hypnosis. 2000;**43**(1):71-75

[61] Tebecis AK, Provins KA, Farnbach RW, Pentony P. Hypnosis and the EEG. A quantitative investigation. The Journal of Nervous and Mental Disease. 1975;**161**(1):1-17

[62] Jensen MP, Sherlin LH, Askew RL, Fregni F, Witkop G, Gianas A, et al. Effects of non-pharmacological pain treatments on brain states. Clinical Neurophysiology. 2013;**124**(10):2016-2024

[63] Williams JD, Gruzelier JH. Differentiation of hypnosis and relaxation by analysis of narrow band theta and alpha frequencies. The International Journal of Clinical and Experimental Hypnosis. 2001;**49**(3):185-206

[64] Corby JC, Roth WT, Zarcone VP Jr, Kopell BS. Psychophysiological correlates of the practice of tantric yoga meditation. Archives of General Psychiatry. 1978;**35**(5):571-577

[65] Perlini AH, Spanos NP. EEG alpha methodologies and hypnotizability: A critical review. Psychophysiology. 1991;**28**(5):511-530. DOI: 10.1111/j.1469-8986.1991.tb01989.x

[66] Pagano RR, Rose RM, Stivers RM, Warrenburg S. Sleep during transcendental meditation. Science. 1976;**191**:308-310

[67] Glicksohn J. The structure of subjective experience: Interdependencies along the sleep-wakefulness continuum. Journal of Mental Imagery. 1989;**13**:99-106

[68] Hebert R, Lehmann D. Theta bursts: An EEG pattern in normal subjects practicing the transcendental meditation technique. Electroencephalography and

Clinical Neurophysiology. 1977;**42**(3):397-405. DOI: 10.1016/0013-4694(1077)90176-90176

[69] Pagano RR, Warrenburg S. Meditation: In search of a unique effect. In: Davidson RJ, Schwartz GE, Shapiro D, editors. Consciousness and Self-Regulation: Advances in Research and Theory. Vol. 3. New York: Plenum; 1983. pp. 153-210

[70] Glicksohn J, Berkovich-Ohana A. Absorption, immersion, and consciousness. In: Gackenbach J, editor. Video Game Play and Consciousness. New York: Nova Science Publishers Inc.; 2012. pp. 83-99

[71] Holroyd J. The science of meditation and the state of hypnosis. The American Journal of Clinical Hypnosis. 2003;**46**(2):109-128

[72] Mitchell DJ, McNaughton N, Flanagan D, Kirk IJ. Frontal-midline theta from the perspective of hippocampal "theta". Progress in Neurobiology. 2008;**86**(3):156-185

[73] Berkovich-Ohana A, Glicksohn J, Goldstein A. Mindfulness-induced changes in gamma band activity—Implications for the default mode network, self-reference and attention. Clinical Neurophysiology. 2012;**123**:700-710. DOI: 10.1016/j.clinph.2011.07.048

[74] Canolty RT, Edwards E, Dalal SS, Soltani M, Nagarajan SS, Kirsch HE, et al. High gamma power is phase-locked to theta oscillations in human neocortex. Science. 2006;**313**(5793):1626-1628

[75] Montgomery SM, Sirota A, Buzsáki G. Theta and gamma coordination of hippocampal networks during waking and rapid eye movement sleep. The Journal of Neuroscience. 2008;**28**(26):6731-6741

[76] Garcia-Rill E, Kezunovic N, Hyde J, Simon C, Beck P, Urbano FJ. Coherence and frequency in the reticular activating system (RAS). Sleep Medicine Reviews. 2013;**17**(3):227-238

[77] Jung-Beeman M, Bowden EM, Haberman J, Frymiare JL, Arambel-Liu S, Greenblatt R, et al. Neural activity when people solve verbal problems with insight. PLoS Biology. 2004;**2**(4):1-15

[78] Jensen MP, Adachi T, Tomé-Pires C, Lee J, Osman ZJ, Miró J. Mechanisms of hypnosis: Toward the development of a biopsychosocial model. The International Journal of Clinical and Experimental Hypnosis. 2015;**63**(1):34-75

[79] Zahedi A, Stuermer B, Hatami J, Rostami R, Sommer W. Eliminating stroop effects with post-hypnotic instructions: Brain mechanisms inferred from EEG. Neuropsychologia. 2017;**96**:70-77

[80] Aftanas LI, Golocheikine SA. Human anterior and frontal midline theta and lower alpha reflect emotionally positive state and internalized attention: High-resolution EEG investigation of meditation. Neuroscience Letters. 2001;**310**(1):57-60

[81] Srinivasan R, Winter WR, Nunez PL. Source analysis of EEG oscillations using high-resolution EEG and MEG. Progress in Brain Research. 2006;**159**:29-42

[82] Whitham EM, Pope KJ, Fitzgibbon SP, Lewis T, Clark CR, Loveless S, et al. Scalp electrical recording during paralysis: Quantitative evidence that EEG frequencies above 20 Hz are contaminated by EMG. Clinical Neurophysiology. 2007;**118**(8):1877-1888

[83] Yuval-Greenberg S, Deouell LY. The broadband-transient induced gamma-band response in scalp EEG reflects the execution of saccades. Brain Topography. 2009;**22**(1):3-6

[84] Kahana MJ, Sekuler R, Caplan JB, Kirschen M, Madsen JR. Human theta oscillations exhibit task dependence during virtual maze navigation. Nature. 1999;**399**(6738):781-784

[85] Buzsáki G. Theta rhythm of navigation: Link between path integration and landmark navigation, episodic and semantic memory. Hippocampus. 2005;**15**(7):827-840

[86] Buzsáki G, Moser EI. Memory, navigation and theta rhythm in the hippocampal-entorhinal system. Nature Neuroscience. 2013;**16**(2):130

[87] Glicksohn J. Cutting the "Gordonian knot" using absorption and dream recall. Journal of Mental Imagery. 1991;**15**(3 & 4):49-54

[88] Glicksohn J. Absorption, hallucinations, and the continuum hypothesis. The Behavioral and Brain Sciences. 2004;**27**(6):793-794

[89] Glicksohn J. Patterns of occurrence of four states of consciousness as a function of trait absorption. Journal for Person-Oriented Research. 2019;**5**(1):27-36

[90] Pekala RJ, Wenger CF, Levine RL. Individual differences in phenomenological experience: States of consciousness as a function of absorption. Journal of Personality and Social Psychology. 1985;**48**(1):125-132. DOI: 10.1037/0022-3514.1048.1031.1125

[91] Qualls PJ, Sheehan PW. Role of the feedback signal in electromyograph biofeedback: The relevance of attention. Journal of Experimental Psychology. General. 1981;**110**(2):204-216. DOI: 10.1037/0096-3445.1110.1032.1204

[92] Tops M, Boksem MAS. Absorbed in the task: Personality measures predict engagement during task performance as tracked by error negativity and asymmetrical frontal activity. Cognitive, Affective, & Behavioral Neuroscience. 2010;**10**(4):441-453

[93] Crawford HJ, Brown AM, Moon CE. Sustained attentional and disattentional abilities: Differences between low and highly hypnotizable persons. Journal of Abnormal Psychology. 1993;**102**(4):534-543. DOI: 10.1037/0021-1843X.1102.1034.1534

[94] Kumar VK, Pekala RJ. Hypnotizability, absorption, and individual differences in phenomenological experience. The International Journal of Clinical and Experimental Hypnosis. 1988;**36**(2):80-88. DOI: 10.1080/00207148808409332

[95] Berkovich-Ohana A, Glicksohn J. Meditation, absorption, transcendent experience and affect: Tying it all together by the consciousness state space (CSS) model. Mindfulness. 2017;**8**:68-77. DOI: 10.1007/s12671-015-0481-9

[96] Silva CE, Kirsch I. Interpretive sets, expectancy, fantasy proneness, and dissociation as predictors of hypnotic response. Journal of Personality and Social Psychology. 1992;**63**(5):847-856. DOI: 10.1037/0022-3514.1063.1035.1847

[97] Council JR, Kirsch I, Hafner LP. Expectancy versus absorption in the prediction of hypnotic responding. Journal of Personality and Social Psychology. 1986;**50**(1):182-189. DOI: 10.1037/0022-3514.1050.1031.1182

[98] Nadon R, Kihlstrom JF, Hoyt IP, Register PA. Absorption and hypnotizability: Context effects reexamined. Journal of Personality and Social Psychology. 1991;**60**(1):144-153. DOI: 10.1037/0022-3514.1060.1031.1144

[99] Mohr C. Are there varying depths in flow? Altered states of consciousness, absorption, and the brain. Journal of Consciousness Studies. 2018;**25**(11-12):115-130

[100] Glicksohn J. Hypnotic behavior revisited: A trait-context interaction. The Behavioral and Brain Sciences. 1987;**10**(4):774-775. DOI: 10.1017/S0140525X00055771

[101] Kihlstrom JF. Neuro-hypnotism: Prospects for hypnosis and neuroscience. Cortex. 2013;**49**(2):365-374

[102] Gruzelier JH. Redefining hypnosis: Theory, methods and integration. Contemporary Hypnosis. 2000;**17**(2):51-70

[103] Graffin NF, Ray WJ, Lundy R. EEG concomitants of hypnosis and hypnotic susceptibility. Journal of Abnormal Psychology. 1995;**104**(1):123-131. DOI: 10.1037/0021-1843X.1104.1031.1123

[104] Schacter DL. EEG theta waves and psychological phenomena: A review and analysis. Biological Psychology. 1977;**5**(1):47-82. DOI: 10.1016/0301-0511(1077)90028-X

[105] White D, Ciorciari J, Carbis C, Liley D. EEG correlates of virtual reality hypnosis. The International Journal of Clinical and Experimental Hypnosis. 2008;**57**(1):94-116

[106] Cardeña E, Jönsson P, Terhune DB, Marcusson-Clavertz D. The neurophenomenology of neutral hypnosis. Cortex. 2013;**49**(2):375-385

[107] van Wijk BC, Daffertshofer A, Roach N, Praamstra P. A role of beta oscillatory synchrony in biasing response competition? Cerebral Cortex. 2009;**19**(6):1294-1302

[108] Roshchina GIA, Koroleva VI, Davydov VI. Changes in the high-frequency electrical brain activity in the animal hypnosis state in rabbits. Zhurnal vysshei nervnoi deiatelnosti imeni I P Pavlova. 2010;**60**(3):352-363

[109] Rusinova EV, Davydov VI. Dynamics of changes in electrical activity in the rabbit cerebral cortex during sequential sessions of "animal hypnosis". Neuroscience and Behavioral Physiology. 2010;**40**(5):471-478

[110] Davidson RJ, Schwartz GE. The psychobiology of relaxation and related states: A multi-process theory. In: Behavior Control and Modification of Physiological Activity. New Jersey: Prentice Hall; 1976. pp. 399-442

[111] Chiesa A, Serretti A. A systematic review of neurobiological and clinical features of mindfulness meditations. Psychological Medicine. 2010;**40**(8):1239-1252

[112] Thomas J, Jamieson G, Cohen M. Low and then high frequency oscillations of distinct right cortical networks are progressively enhanced by medium and long term Satyananda yoga meditation practice. Frontiers in Human Neuroscience. 2014;**8**:197

[113] Lehmann D, Faber P, Achermann P, Jeanmonod D, Gianotti L, Pizzagalli D. Brain sources of EEG gamma frequency during volitionally meditation-induced, altered states of consciousness, and experience of the self. Psychiatry Research. 2001;**108**:111-121. DOI: 10.1016/S0925-4927(01)00116-0

[114] Lutz A, Greischar LL, Rawlings NB, Ricard M, Davidson RJ. Long-term meditators self-induce high-amplitude gamma synchrony during mental practice. Proceedings of the National Academy of Sciences of the United States of America. 2004;**101**:16369-16373. DOI: 10.1073/pnas.0407401101

[115] Ivanovski B, Malhi GS. The psychological and neurophysiological concomitants of mindfulness forms of meditation. Acta Neuropsychiatrica. 2007;**19**(2):76-91

[116] Berman AE, Stevens L. EEG manifestations of nondual experiences

in meditators. Consciousness and Cognition. 2015;**31**:1-11

[117] Berkovich-OhanaA,Dor-ZidermanY, Glicksohn J, Goldstein A. Alterations in the sense of time, space, and body in the mindfulness-trained brain: A neurophenomenologically-guided MEG study. Frontiers in Psychology. 2013;**4**:912

[118] Berkovich-Ohana A, Glicksohn J, Ben-Soussan TD, Goldstein A. Creativity is enhanced by long-term mindfulness training and is negatively correlated with trait default-mode-related low-gamma inter-hemispheric connectivity. Mindfulness. 2017;**8**(3):717-727

[119] Knyazev GG. EEG delta oscillations as a correlate of basic homeostatic and motivational processes. Neuroscience and Biobehavioral Reviews. 2012;**36**(1):677-695

[120] Ben-Soussan TD, Mauro F, Lasaponara S, Glicksohn J, Marson F, Berkovich-Ohana A. Fully immersed: State absorption and electrophysiological effects of the OVO whole-body perceptual deprivation chamber. Progress in Brain Research. 2019;**244**:165-184

[121] Parker S, Bharati SV, Fernandez M. Defining yoga-nidra: Traditional accounts, physiological research, and future directions. International Journal of Yoga Therapy. 2013;**23**(1):11-16

[122] Dennison P. The human default consciousness and its disruption: Insights from an EEG study of Buddhist jhāna meditation. Frontiers in Human Neuroscience. 2019;**13**:178

[123] Del Felice A, Arcaro C, Storti SF, Fiaschi A, Manganotti P. Electrical source imaging of sleep spindles. Clinical EEG and Neuroscience. 2014;**45**:184-192. DOI: 10.1177/1550059413497716

[124] Mason LI, Alexander CN, Travis FT, Marsh G, Orme-Johnson DW, Gackenbach J, et al. Electrophysiological correlates of higher states of consciousness during sleep in long-term: Practitioners of the transcendental meditation program. Sleep. 1997;**20**(2):102-110

[125] Travis F. Transcendental experiences during meditation practice. Annals of the New York Academy of Sciences. 2014;**1307**(1):1-8

[126] Asada H, Fukuda Y, Tsunoda S, Yamaguchi M, Tonoike M. Frontal midline theta rhythms reflect alternative activation of prefrontal cortex and anterior cingulate cortex in humans. Neuroscience Letters. 1999;**274**(1):29-32

[127] Gevins A, Smith ME, McEvoy L, Yu D. High-resolution EEG mapping of cortical activation related to working memory: Effects of task difficulty, type of processing, and practice. Cerebral Cortex. 1997;**7**(4):374-385

[128] Ishii R, Shinosaki K, Ukai S, Inouye T, Ishihara T, Yoshimine T, et al. Medial prefrontal cortex generates frontal midline theta rhythm. Neuroreport. 1999;**10**(4):675-679

[129] Mizuhara H et al. A long-range cortical network emerging with theta oscillation in a mental task. Neuroreport. 2004;**15**(8):1233-1238

[130] Sammer G et al. Relationship between regional hemodynamic activity and simultaneously recorded EEG-theta associated with mental arithmetic-induced workload. Human Brain Mapping. 2007;**28**(8):793-803

[131] Onton J, Delorme A, Makeig S. Frontal midline EEG dynamics during working memory. NeuroImage. 2005;**27**(2):341-356

[132] Menon V. Salience network. In: Toga W, editor. Brain Mapping. An Encyclopedic Reference. Vol. 2.

New York: Academic Press, Elsevier; 2015. pp. 597-711

[133] Menon V, Uddin LQ. Saliency, switching, attention and control: A network model of insula function. Brain Structure & Function. 2010;**214**:655-667. DOI: 10.1007/s00429-010-0262-0

[134] Murayama K, Matsumoto M, Izuma K, Matsumoto K. Neural basis of the undermining effect of monetary reward on intrinsic motivation. Proceedings of the National Academy of Sciences of the United States of America. 2010;**107**(49):20911-20916

[135] Brewer JA, Worhunsky PD, Gray JR, Tang YY, Weber J, Kober H. Meditation experience is associated with differences in default mode network activity and connectivity. Proceedings of the National Academy of Sciences of the United States of America. 2011;**108**(50):20254-20259

[136] Farb N, Segal Z, Mayberg H, Bean J, McKeon D, Fatima Z, et al. Attending to the present: Mindfulness meditation reveals distinct neural modes of self-reference. Social Cognitive and Affective Neuroscience. 2007;**2**:313-322. DOI: 10.1093/scan/nsm030

[137] Hölzel B, Ott U, Hempel H, Hackl A, Wolf K, Stark R, et al. Differential engagement of anterior cingulate and adjacent medial frontal cortex in adept meditators and non-meditators. Neuroscience Letters. 2007;**421**:16-21. DOI: 10.1016/j.neulet.2007.04.074

[138] Deeley Q, Oakley DA, Toone B, Giampietro V, Brammer MJ, Williams SCR, et al. Modulating the default mode network using hypnosis. The International Journal of Clinical and Experimental Hypnosis. 2012;**60**:206-228. DOI: 10.1080/00207144.2012.648070

[139] Lifshitz M, Cusumano EP, Raz A. Hypnosis as neurophenomenology. Frontiers in Human Neuroscience. 2013;7:469

[140] Crabbe JB, Dishman RK. Brain electrocortical activity during and after exercise: A quantitative synthesis. Psychophysiology. 2004;**41**(4):563-574

[141] Gutmann B, Hülsdünker T, Mierau J, Strüder HK, Mierau A. Exercise-induced changes in EEG alpha power depend on frequency band definition mode. Neuroscience Letters. 2018;**662**:271-275

[142] Babiloni C, Marzano N, Iacoboni M, Infarinato F, Aschieri P, Buffo P, et al. Resting state cortical rhythms in athletes: A high-resolution EEG study. Brain Research Bulletin. 2010;**81**(1):149-156

[143] Dietrich A. Functional neuroanatomy of altered states of consciousness: The transient hypofrontality hypothesis. Consciousness and Cognition. 2003;**12**(2):231-256. DOI: 10.1016/S1053-8100(1002)00046-00046

[144] Dietrich A, Audiffren M. The reticular-activating hypofrontality (RAH) model of acute exercise. Neuroscience and Biobehavioral Reviews. 2011;**35**(6):1305-1325

[145] Voss DE. Proprioceptive neuromuscular facilitation. American Journal of Physical Medicine & Rehabilitation. 1967;**46**(1):838-898

[146] Diamond A. Effects of physical exercise on executive functions: Going beyond simply moving to moving with thought. Annals of Sports Medicine and Research. 2015;**2**(1):1011

[147] De Bono E. Information processing and new ideas—Lateral and vertical thinking. The Journal of Creative Behavior. 1969;**3**(3):159-171

[148] Shapiro F. Eye movement desensitization: A new treatment for

post-traumatic stress disorder. Journal of Behavior Therapy and Experimental Psychiatry. 1989;**20**(3):211-217

[149] Shapiro FE, editor. EMDR as an Integrative Psychotherapy Approach: Experts of Diverse Orientations Explore the Paradigm Prism. Washington: American Psychological Association; 2002. pp. 7-444

[150] Nishida M, Pearsall J, Buckner RL, Walker MP. REM sleep, prefrontal theta, and the consolidation of human emotional memory. Cerebral Cortex. 2009;**19**(5):1158-1166

[151] Stickgold R. EMDR: A putative neurobiological mechanism of action. Journal of Clinical Psychology. 2002;**58**(1):61-75

[152] Stickgold R. Sleep-dependent memory processing and EMDR action. Journal of EMDR Practice and Research. 2008;**2**:289-299. DOI: 10.1891/1933-3196.2.4.289

[153] Pagani M, Amann BL, Landin-Romero R, Carletto S. Eye movement desensitization and reprocessing and slow wave sleep: A putative mechanism of action. Frontiers in Psychology. 2017;**8**:1935

[154] Brady B, Stevens L. Binaural-beat induced theta EEG activity and hypnotic susceptibility. The American Journal of Clinical Hypnosis. 2000;**43**(1):53-69

[155] Jirakittayakorn N, Wongsawat Y. Brain responses to a 6-Hz binaural beat: Effects on general theta rhythm and frontal midline theta activity. Frontiers in Neuroscience. 2017;**11**:365

[156] McConnell PA, Froeliger B, Garland EL, Ives JC, Sforzo GA. Auditory driving of the autonomic nervous system: Listening to theta-frequency binaural beats post-exercise increases parasympathetic activation and sympathetic withdrawal. Frontiers in Psychology. 2014;**5**:1248

[157] Crawford HJ, Gruzelier JH. A midstream view of the neuropsychology of hypnosis: Recent research and future directions. In: Fromm E, Nash MR, editors. Contemporary Hypnosis Research. New York: Guilford Press; 1992. pp. 227-266

[158] Solca M, Mottaz A, Guggisberg AG. Binaural beats increase interhemispheric alpha-band coherence between auditory cortices. Hearing Research. 2016;**332**:233-237

[159] Adrian ED. The Physical Background of Perception. Oxford: Clarendon Press; 1948. p. 95

[160] Von Stein A, Sarnthein J. Different frequencies for different scales of cortical integration: From local gamma to long range alpha/theta synchronization. International Journal of Psychophysiology. 2000;**38**(3):301-313

[161] Marson F, Paoletti P, Lasaponara S, Glicksohn J, De Fano A, Ben-Soussan TD. Cerebral spectral perturbation during upper limbs diagonal movements. In: Ramana V, editor. Advances in Neural Signal Processing. [In press]

[162] Parkes LM, Bastiaansen MC, Norris DG. Combining EEG and fMRI to investigate the post-movement beta rebound. NeuroImage. 2006;**29**(3):685-696

[163] De Fano A, Leshem R, Ben-Soussan TD. Creating an internal environment of cognitive and psycho-emotional well-being through an external movement-based environment: An overview of quadrato motor training. International Journal of Environmental Research and Public Health. 2019;**16**(12):2160

[164] Leshem R, De Fano A, Ben-Soussan TD. The implications of motor and cognitive inhibition for hot and cool executive functions: The case of quadrato motor training. Frontiers in Psychology. (in press)

[165] Piervincenzi C, Ben-Soussan TD, Mauro F, Mallio CA, Errante Y, Quattrocchi CC, et al. White matter microstructural changes following quadrato motor training: A longitudinal study. Frontiers in Human Neuroscience. 2017;**11**:590

[166] Pfurtscheller G, Da Silva FL. Event-related EEG/MEG synchronization and desynchronization: Basic principles. Clinical Neurophysiology. 1999;**110**(11):1842-1857

[167] Kilavik BE, Zaepffel M, Brovelli A, MacKay WA, Riehle A. The ups and downs of beta oscillations in sensorimotor cortex. Experimental Neurology. 2013;**245**:15-26

[168] Ben-Soussan TD, Berkovich-Ohana A, Glicksohn J, Goldstein A. A suspended act: Increased reflectivity and gender-dependent electrophysiological change following quadrato motor training. Frontiers in Psychology. 2014;**5**:55. DOI: 10.3389/fpsyg.2014.00055

[169] Lasaponara S, Mauro F, Ben-Soussan TD, Carducci F, Tombini M, Quattrocchi CC, et al. Electrophysiological indexes of eyes open and closed resting states conditions following the quadrato motor training. International Journal of Bioelectromagnetism. 2016; **18**:99-108

[170] Ben-Soussan TD, Avirame K, Glicksohn J, Goldstein A, Harpaz Y, Ben-Schachar M. Changes in cerebellar activity and inter-hemispheric coherence accompany improved reading capacity following quadrato motor training. Frontiers in Systems Neuroscience. 2014;**8**:81. DOI: 10.3389/fnsys.2014.00081

[171] Lasaponara S, Mauro F, Carducci F, Paoletti P, Tombini M, Quattrocchi CC, et al. Increased alpha band functional connectivity following the quadrato motor training: A longitudinal study. Frontiers in Human Neuroscience. 2017;**11**:282

[172] Ben-Soussan T, Glicksohn J, Goldstein A, Berkovich-Ohana A, Donchin O. Into the square and out of the box: The effects of quadrato motor training on creativity and alpha coherence. PLoS One. 2013;**8**:e55023

[173] Ben-Soussan TD, Glicksohn J, Ohana AB, Donchin O, Goldstein A. Step in time: Changes in EEG coherence during a time estimation task following quadrato motor training. In: Proceedings of the 27th Annual Meeting of the International Society for Psychophysics; 24-27 October 2011; Herzliya, Israel. Vol. 27. pp. 239-244

[174] Engel AK, Fries P. Neuronal oscillations, coherence, and consciousness. In: Laureys S, Gosseries O, Tononi G, editors. The Neurology of Consciousness. 2nd ed. Amsterdam, The Netherlands: Elsevier; 2016. pp. 49-60

[175] Sauseng P, Klimesch W, Schabus M, Doppelmayr M. Fronto-parietal EEG coherence in theta and upper alpha reflect central executive functions of working memory. International Journal of Psychophysiology. 2005;**57**:97-103

[176] Travis F, Tecce J, Arenander A, Wallace RK. Patterns of EEG coherence, power, and contingent negative variation characterize the integration of transcendental and waking states. Biological Psychology. 2002;**61**:293-319

[177] Bennett IJ, Motes MA, Rao NK, Rypma B. White matter tract integrity predicts visual search performance in

young and older adults. Neurobiology of Aging. 2012;**33**(2):433-e21

[178] Pan W, Zhang L, Xia Y. The difference in EEG theta waves between concentrative and non-concentrative qigong states—A power spectrum and topographic mapping study. Journal of Traditional Chinese Medicine. 1994;**14**(3):212-218

[179] Field T, Diego M, Hernandez-Reif M. Tai chi/yoga effects on anxiety, heartrate, EEG and math computations. Complementary Therapies in Clinical Practice. 2010;**16**(4):235-238

[180] Liu Y, Mimura K, Wang L, Ikuda K. Physiological benefits of 24-style Taijiquan exercise in middle-aged women. Journal of Physiological Anthropology and Applied Human Science. 2003;**22**:219-225. DOI: 10.2114/jpa.22.219

[181] Ambrose KR, Yvonne MG. Physical exercise as non-pharmacological treatment of chronic pain: Why and when. Best Practice & Research. Clinical Rheumatology. 2015;**29**(1):120-130

[182] Peng PWH. Tai chi and chronic pain. Regional Anesthesia and Pain Medicine. 2012;**37**:372-382

[183] Farb NA, Desormeau PA, Dinh-Williams LA. The neuroscience of hypo-egoic processes. In: The Oxford Handbook of Hypo-egoic Phenomena. 2016. pp. 109-131

[184] Llinás RR. I of the Vortex: From Neurons to Self. Cambridge, Massachusetts, London, England: MIT Press; 2002. p. 320

[185] Pesce C, Ben-Soussan TD. "Cogito ergo sum" or "ambulo ergo sum"? New perspectives in developmental exercise and cognition research. In: McMorris T, editor. Exercise-Cognition Interaction: Neuroscience Perspectives. Elsevier Academic Press; 2016. pp. 251-282. DOI: 10.1016/B978-0-12-800778-5.00012-8

[186] Chiesa A. The difficulty of defining mindfulness: Current thought and critical issues. Mindfulness. 2013;**4**(3):255-268

[187] Lutz A, Jha AP, Dunne JD, Saron CD. Investigating the phenomenological matrix of mindfulness-related practices from a neurocognitive perspective. The American Psychologist. 2015;**70**(7):632

[188] Dienes Z, Lush P, Semmens-Wheeler R, Parkinson J, Scott R, Naish P. Hypnosis as self-deception; meditation as self-insight. In: Hypnosis and Meditation: Toward an Integrative Science of Conscious Planes. Oxford, United Kingdom: Oxford University Press; 2016. pp. 107-128

[189] Kirsch I. The social learning theory of hypnosis. In: Lynn SJ, Rhue JW, editors. Theories of Hypnosis: Current Models and Perspectives. New York: Guildford Press; 1991. pp. 439-466

[190] Babiloni C, Vecchio F, Bares M, Brazdil M, Nestrasil I, Eusebi F, et al. Functional coupling between anterior prefrontal cortex (BA10) and hand muscle contraction during intentional and imitative motor acts. NeuroImage. 2008;**39**(3):1314-1323

[191] Mölle M, Marshall L, Gais S, Born J. Grouping of spindle activity during slow oscillations in human non-rapid eye movement sleep. The Journal of Neuroscience. 2002;**22**(24):10941-10947

[192] Hilgard ER, Hilgard JR. Hypnosis in the Relief of Pain. New York, London: Routledge; 2013. p. 312

[193] Rissacher D, Dowman R, Schuckers SAC. Identifying frequency-domain features for an EEG-based pain measurement system. In: Proceedings

of 2007 IEEE 33rd Annual Northeast Bioengineering Conference. New York: IEEE; 2007. pp. 114-115

[194] Hsiao FJ, Wang SJ, Lin YY, Fuh JL, Ko YC, Wang PN, et al. Altered insula-default mode network connectivity in fibromyalgia: A resting-state magnetoencephalographic study. The Journal of Headache and Pain. 2017;**18**(1):89

[195] Sullivan MJ, Sullivan ME, Adams HM. Stage of chronicity and cognitive correlates of pain-related disability. Cognitive Behaviour Therapy. 2002;**31**(3):111-118

[196] Hamilton JP, Furman DJ, Chang C, Thomason ME, Dennis E, Gotlib IH. Default-mode and task-positive network activity in major depressive disorder: Implications for adaptive and maladaptive rumination. Biological Psychiatry. 2011;**70**(4):327-333

[197] King AP, Block SR, Sripada RK, Rauch S, Giardino N, Favorite T, et al. Altered default mode network (DMN) resting state functional connectivity following a mindfulness-based exposure therapy for posttraumatic stress disorder (PTSD) in combat veterans of Afghanistan and Iraq. Depression and Anxiety. 2016;**33**(4):289-299

[198] Kucyi A, Moayedi M, Weissman-Fogel I, Goldberg MB, Freeman BV, Tenenbaum HC, et al. Enhanced medial prefrontal-default mode network functional connectivity in chronic pain and its association with pain rumination. The Journal of Neuroscience. 2014;**34**(11):3969-3975

[199] Shim M, Im CH, Lee SH. Disrupted cortical brain network in post-traumatic stress disorder patients: A resting-state electroencephalographic study. Translational Psychiatry. 2017;7(9):e1231-e1231

[200] Cunningham NR, Kashikar-Zuck S, Coghill RC. Brain mechanisms impacted by psychological therapies for pain: Identifying targets for optimization of treatment effects. Pain Reports. 2019;**4**:4

[201] Zeidan F, Grant JA, Brown CA, McHaffie JG, Coghill RC. Mindfulness meditation-related pain relief: Evidence for unique brain mechanisms in the regulation of pain. Neuroscience Letters. 2012;**520**(2):165-173

[202] Lutz A, McFarlin DR, Perlman DM, Salomons TV, Davidson RJ. Altered anterior insula activation during anticipation and experience of painful stimuli in expert meditators. NeuroImage. 2013;**64**:538-546

[203] Sivertsen M, Normann B. Embodiment and self in reorientation to everyday life following severe traumatic brain injury. Physiotherapy Theory and Practice. 2015;**31**(3):153-159

[204] Klemm WR. Neurophysiologic studies of the immobility reflex ("animal hypnosis"). In: Neurosciences Research. New York, London: Academic Press; 1971. pp. 165-212

[205] Gallup GG Jr. Animal hypnosis: Factual status of a fictional concept. Psychological Bulletin. 1974;**81**(11):836

[206] Braboszcz C, Delorme A. Lost in thoughts: Neural markers of low alertness during mind wandering. NeuroImage. 2011;**54**(4):3040-3047

[207] Nash MR, Barnier AJ, editors. The Oxford Handbook of Hypnosis: Theory, Research, and Practice. Oxford, United Kingdom: Oxford University Press; 2012. p. 802. DOI: 10.1093/oxfordhb/9780198570097.001.0001

[208] Tart C. Waking up: Overcoming the obstacles to human potential. Lucidity Letter. Boston: New Science Library; 1986;5(2):307

Section 3

Novalties in Hypnotherapeutic Applications

Chapter 5

Cognitive Hypnotherapy

Elizabeth Brooker

Abstract

Cognitive hypnotherapy (CH) is an assimilative therapy rooted in cognitive therapy and behavioural therapy, with the addition of hypnosis. It is a psychodynamic therapy that focuses on the unconscious mind (implicit thoughts, actions and emotions) no longer in conscious awareness. This chapter gives a brief synopsis of the hypnotic procedures and protocols that are most pertinent for understanding the case for integration. It gives the background of cognitive behavioural therapy (CBT) and a brief history of how this therapy evolved. It further gives the rationale for the integration of hypnosis with CBT, corroborated with evidence from the literature. CH treatments are documented in some detail in a number of different domains where hypnosis is used as an adjunct to therapy for the treatment of debilitating psychological conditions. The techniques and procedures are designed to desensitise and reprocess dysfunctional cognitions, emotions and memories enabling positive change in cognitive perceptions and visualisation. The author, an academic and experienced clinical practitioner of CH for more than 10 years, recognises that there is much scepticism regarding this therapy. It is hoped that this review will give greater understanding and more credence to this highly effective therapy in both the scientific community and medical profession.

Keywords: cognitive hypnotherapy, hypnosis, unconscious mind, psychodynamic therapy, CBT

1. Introduction

Cognitive hypnotherapy (CH), rooted in cognitive behavioural therapy (CBT) with the addition of hypnosis, focuses on the ways in which individuals think and act in specific circumstances, and how emotional and behavioural problems may be overcome. The fusion of hypnotic techniques with the cognitive and behavioural therapies was proposed in 1994 to strengthen the therapeutic outcome and was termed cognitive hypnotherapy. This offered an addition to therapy by facilitating the resolution of resistant symptoms [1]. CH is a psychodynamic therapy that focuses on the unconscious mind and targets implicit or automated processes (thoughts and feelings) no longer consciously perceived.

The aim of this review is to give greater understanding of CH and its quick-acting and beneficial effects in a number of diverse conditions. A further aim is to give corroborated scientific evidence from the literature of the processes adopted in this assimilative therapy underpinned by documentation of studies in a number of different areas. The objective is to give more credence and understanding of CH in both the scientific and medical domains.

This chapter first asks the question 'what is hypnosis'? and gives an overview from a scientific stand-point of the techniques and protocols of hypnosis that are most pertinent for understanding the case for integration with CBT. It gives a brief review of the background of CBT from its roots in cognitive therapy and behavioural therapy. It further evaluates the nature and efficacy of CBT together with its suitability from a psychological perspective as an appropriate therapy for the addition of hypnosis. The impact and added strength of integrating two disciplines for the maximum therapeutic effect is explored, together with the rationale for integration. Documentation is given of scientific studies in a number of different domains where hypnosis has been used as an adjunct to CBT and the treatment effects of this multi-modal approach. However this chapter concludes with the premise that there appear to be few guidelines for practitioners for an integrative procedure for the treatment of diverse psychological conditions and this needs to be addressed in future research.

2. What is hypnosis?

Hypnosis dates back more than 220 years as an area of scientific research and clinical practice and is used to bring about positive change in a wide variety of conditions. It has been suggested that in a trance-like state, as in hypnosis, a process of communication with the unconscious mind occurs. This results in an unconscious response to suggestion [2] allowing individuals to relax deeply. In fact trance has been described as a natural state of mind that is entered into without realising, as in daydreaming [3]. While in trance the therapist attempts to address the subject's unconscious mind; selective thinking of positive thoughts is established, substituting former judgemental cognitions with helpful ones [4]. Cognitive psychology deals with the meaning of events, the underlying processes and ways of structuring and interpreting experiences. It encompasses affect, perception and behaviour [5]. It is reported that during trance, behaviour may be altered, enabling subjects to re-associate and reorganise inner psychological complexities [2]. Perceptions can be changed and negative cognitions supplanted by positive ideas. The unconscious mind is reprogrammed, allowing the individual in the conscious state the freedom to act and carry out new, positive subjective ideas. In fact, breakthroughs relating to the neurobiology of emotion and the endocrinology of stress are providing new data for conceptualising learning and behaviour as one of the major psychological foundations of therapeutic hypnosis [4].

It has been proposed that hypnosis is based on the affect theory of human emotion and that through the use of specific language they (hypnosis and cognitive therapy) are based on similar ideas of affect [6]. In fact, it is suggested that intransigent symptoms of dysfunctional cognitions and emotions are approached and treated in cognitive therapy through a sequence of interactions similar to hypnosis, as thoughts previously locked to negative affect are processed positively. The literature further suggests that cognitions locked to unpleasant emotions can become disturbingly resistant to change until hypnosis alters the affective perceptions of the individual [6]. It is argued that psychotherapeutic interventions can effect substantial change in the affective, behavioural and cognitive areas of the brain [7]. Hypnosis itself is not a therapy; however it is suggested that when used as an adjunct to therapy the hypnotic relationship enhances the efficacy of the treatment effects [8].

In the current review, Ericksonian Hypnotherapy is critiqued as this technique uses a set of procedures designed to alter the state of consciousness. Ericksonian philosophy emphasises the ability of individuals to access their own resources to improve the quality of their lives, recontextualising the memory, the effect of fear and physiological hyper-arousal. It has been suggested that during this state the memory and meaning of negative experiences can be changed through emotional processing, as well as decreasing the somatic symptoms of anxiety associated with the event [9–11].

2.1 The techniques and protocols of hypnosis

The following is a brief synopsis of the techniques and protocols of hypnosis with corroboration of these statements taken from the literature:

Hypnosis enhances the effectiveness of therapy and creates the belief of self-efficacy [12]. Evidence from the literature informs us that perceived self-efficacy not only creates a sense of hope but also affects the treatment [13], and that expectation of self-efficacy is central to all forms of therapeutic change [14].

Hypnosis adds leverage to treatment and shortens treatment time [15]. When patients are fully relaxed, positive subjective experiences occur replacing negative cognitions, which appear to bring great comfort and relief [16]. Rapid changes are attributed to the brisk and profound behavioural, emotional, cognitive and physiological changes brought about by hypnosis [17].

Hypnosis breaks resistance when indirect hypnotic suggestions are applied in therapy [18]. Oppositional statements given by the therapist are used to obtain compliance. An example of this would be 'and the more you try to open your eyes the more they remain tightly shut'. The word 'try' pre-disposes failure, so it is used in therapy whenever the opposite is required [18].

Hypnosis facilitates rapid transference, which reinforces the suggestions given in therapy. *During hypnosis, there is greater access to fantasies, memories and emotions, allowing the rapid occurrence of full-blown transference manifestations* [19]. During the hypnotic state, the critical faculty of the mind is bypassed, enabling the processing of thoughts in the unconscious mind, which are then transferred to the conscious in the waking state [4].

Hypnosis induces deep relaxation, and in this state suggestions can be made that are effective for the reduction of anxiety [10]. A trance is a special psychological state in which patients can re-associate and reorganise their inner psychological complexities. It is argued that during therapy an inner resynthesis of the patient's behaviour is achieved by the patient [4], and further argued that suggestion and post-hypnotic suggestions during therapy emphasise the innate tendency of the mind to heal itself [20].

Hypnosis strengthens the ego by enhancing self-confidence and self-worth [21]. Ego strengthening is a belief that when positive suggestions are repeated sufficiently they become embedded in the unconscious mind to be acted upon in the conscious state [22].

Hypnosis facilitates divergent thinking, maximising awareness, attentional focus and concentration. It minimises distraction and interference from other sources and stimuli increasing the potential for learning alternatives [23]. Corroboration from the literature reports that breaking through the limitations of conscious attitudes frees the unconscious potential for problem-solving [4].

Hypnosis allows engagement of the non-dominant hemisphere in the brain. It provides direct entry into the cognitive processing of the right cerebral hemisphere (in right-handed subjects), which accesses and organises emotional and experiential information. It can be utilised to teach restructuring of cognitive and emotional processes that are influenced by the non-dominant cerebral hemisphere [22]. Many of the sensory-perceptual languages of the mind (visual, auditory and kinaesthetic information) are encoded like a map over the cerebral cortex of the brain [24, 25].

Hypnosis facilitates imagery conditioning. In this state, imagery and cognitive restructuring are intensified. The use of the word 'hypnosis' and the application of various hypnotic techniques appear to augment the power of the suggestion [26]. Evidence from the literature suggests that when the patient is hypnotised, the power of imagination is increased and that possibly hypnosis, imagery and affect are all mediated by the same right cerebral hemisphere [27].

Hypnosis uses post-hypnotic suggestions and is an important part of therapy and is used to shape desired future behaviour; it can be powerful in altering problem behaviours, dysfunctional cognitions and negative emotions [28]. It is reported that post-hypnotic suggestions function as positive ideas for desired future behaviour, and are regarded as a necessary part of the therapeutic process, enabling the patient to act upon the suggestions in future experiences [16].

Hypnosis enhances training in positive self-hypnosis, which provides a strategy for counteracting negative cognitions [29]. It is argued that negative thinking can lead to negative affect, biased thoughts, impaired motivation, concentration and cognition [30]. Positive techniques can be practised during self-hypnosis, thus reinforcing and strengthening hypnotherapy.

Hypnotic techniques are easily exported and can be easily assimilated with many forms of therapy. When hypnosis is used as an adjunct to a particular form of therapy whether behavioural, cognitive or cognitive behavioural therapy, the effects can enhance the treatment outcome [12].

The above techniques and protocols suggest that by adopting hypnosis as an adjunct to therapy addressing the unconscious mind, change can be implemented quickly, is more profound and therapy outcome is enhanced. By adopting this therapeutic procedure, it follows that therapy outcome should be more effective than CBT alone. An overview of the background of CBT is now given together with the rationale for the integration of CBT with hypnosis.

3. The background of CBT

3.1 Cognitive therapy

Cognitive therapy is organised around the idea that behaviour is based on schemas and that these are shaped by early experiences. Schematic thoughts consist of memories, attitudes, core beliefs and assumptions and are factors that, when occurring in certain circumstances, can result in individuals spiralling into negativity and consequential psychological problems [31]. Implicit memories (memories no longer consciously perceived) and explicit negative memories of past experiences can trigger latent patterns of thoughts, emotions and behaviour, resulting in a vicious cycle that maintains and exacerbates the non-helpful behaviour. It is argued that implicit memory is the unconscious remembering of thoughts that accompanied specific events. If negative thoughts have been encoded, implicit feelings are brought into conscious awareness causing both physiological and psychological symptoms [32]. It has been concluded that interventions should focus on problematic over-activation of safety behaviours [33]. This research was extended when the common elements in different anxiety disorders (dysfunctional thinking, physiological reactions, and behavioural responses based on the 'fight or flight syndrome', the body's reaction to unpleasant experiences) were reviewed, and a process map of treatment formulated enabling therapists to adhere to a treatment plan [34].

3.2 Behavioural therapy

Behavioural therapy, in contrast to cognitive therapy, is based on the premise that undesirable behaviours are learned and as such can be 'unlearned' through a process of systematic desensitisation. It is argued that desired behaviours can be taught and reinforced and unwanted behaviours eliminated [35]. Behavioural therapy was expanded when the theory of shaping behaviour by a system of rewards and punishment was first postulated [36]. Behavioural theorists consider that specific phobias and anxiety conditions are acquired through a process of classical conditioning, and that all learned responses derive from innate behavioural patterns, the stimulus/response paradigm [37]. The basis of behavioural therapy encouraged therapists to use techniques aimed at changing the negative affect, introducing positive cognitions through the use of language [38].

While behavioural therapy is based primarily on learning theory and cognitive therapy is rooted more in cognitive theory, the two systems have much in common [39]. Both behavioural and cognitive therapy focus on changing dysfunctional behaviour that occurs in feared situations and both concentrate on positive visual imagery of the environment and situation in which the maladaptive behaviour occurs. Other commonalities are management of physiological and somatic symptoms of anxiety and verbal-assisted coping strategies. However, there are differences in the techniques used in each therapy: the behaviourists concentrate on systematic desensitisation and sequencing of negative images [40], whereas cognitive therapists target the patient's unhelpful reported thoughts [39]. However, the methodologies of behavioural therapists were integrated with cognitive therapies, resulting in a heterogeneous set of techniques and procedures that distinguished between conscious beliefs and unconscious representations in memory [41]. This was a new concept developed from behavioural therapy and became known as cognitive behavioural therapy, resulting in specific cognitive behavioural treatments being developed for a variety of psychological problems [42].

3.3 Cognitive behavioural therapy (CBT)

Since the 1960s, cognitive behavioural theory has gained popularity. CBT uses a combination of behavioural and cognitive interventions aimed at changing negative thinking patterns and behaviours and is one of the most researched psychological interventions [43]. CBT is frequently used in the clinical environment and its practice is evidence-based. It focuses on the way individuals think and act in specific circumstances and how emotional and behavioural problems may be overcome. It adopts a formulation of protocols and procedures that are used to treat psychological conditions, and enables development of flexible realistic beliefs [22]. Individuals are helped in the pursuit of goals, and emotional problems are aided and overcome by directing cognitions towards memories, images, thoughts and attention [42].

Specific patterns of thinking are associated with a range of psychological problems and through its development, CBT has adopted treatments for anxiety conditions and emotional disorders such as depression, generalised anxiety disorder, panic disorder, post-traumatic stress and specific phobias [44]. There are a number of distinctive diktats and protocols that contribute to an effective model of CBT. Various longitudinal formulations have been devised to aid the management and treatment of problems. However, for the purpose of this review, the formulation devised by Persons [45] is used, as this diagram is most usually associated with CBT and bridges the gap between behavioural and cognitive formulations [38]. An adaptation of the diagram illustrates the relationship to the root cause and effect of anxiety.

Persons' Formulation (1989)

Early Experience: Negative experience either from teacher, parents or peers.

↓

Schemas: Become maladjusted and lead to mistrust. Mistrusts ability to do things.

Core Beliefs: Negative cognitions result in anxiety leading to behavioural and physiological problems.

↓

Assumptions: I know I will feel anxious because it always happens and then I will .... (becomes a self-fulfilling prophecy).

↓

Trigger: Thought of an impending event.

↓

Vicious cycle:

Negative Automatic Thought (NAT): Negative thoughts of dread, apprehension and failure.

↑ ↓

Consequence: The conceptualised belief regarding the event is realised.

Feeling: Hopelessness, worthlessness, depression, shame and withdrawal.

↑ ↓

Behaviour: Decision not to put themselves in that situation again.

Working on the supposition that the way an individual thinks and feels largely determines the outcome of the personal experience, CBT helps to redress negative cognitions. It is reported in the literature that CBT is cognitively orientated to future events, and encourages the association of specific positive thoughts, feelings and behaviour in a particular context [38]. Through changing beliefs and self-help, individuals are encouraged to change negativity into positive outcomes [22]. Goal-orientated ideas and suppositions are reiterated, aimed at strengthening the ego, making strong links through visualisation and imaginings. Corrected thoughts enable the handling of situations and feelings in such a way that a positive outcome is achieved and anxiety reduced [4].

However, the literature reports that no theory/therapeutic action is without flaws, and a number of issues have been identified with the CBT approach: the failure to consider experiences in the past in relation to the present in generating anxiety; the effective role that cognition plays on physiological symptoms in the body; the failure to recognise the role of the unconscious mind in overt behaviour; and the failure to recognise that human thought and action are socially embedded [46]. Further to this, evidence from the literature indicates that one of the main drawbacks with CBT is the number of sessions required to effect positive change (10 or more sessions in some cases) [47].

Practitioners of hypnosis often employ techniques used by CBT therapists [48]. However, the protocols and procedures adapted by hypnotherapists explore past and present negative experiences in relation to the presenting problem, together with the effect of cognitions on physiological and behavioural outcomes [47]. It is argued that the addition of these protocols with the added impact of hypnosis incorporated with CBT is a means of enabling a quicker and stronger resolution to the clinical condition [22]. There now follows a description of the suitability of hypnosis being used as an adjunct to CBT therapy.

4. Assimilating hypnotic techniques with CBT: rationale for integration

4.1 Assimilation

The following is evidence from the literature for the potential assimilative practice of hypnosis with CBT.

It has been suggested that as a result of incorporating techniques from another approach into one's own main theoretical domain, the core ideas of the former are integrated into the latter (or 'host' theory), changing both and resulting in a new assimilative integrative model [49]. Multimodal therapy was first used when hypnotic techniques were incorporated into behavioural procedures, and hypnosis was used with psychoanalysis [13]. There are many reasons for assimilating hypnotic techniques with CBT, which are beneficial to both therapists and patients. Change in any one area will lead to changes in other areas as patient and therapist consider thoughts, bodily feelings, emotions and actions [50]. The use of hypnosis can also be used as a means of empowerment in new and creative ways. Social psychological theories of hypnosis suggest that the major mechanism mediating hypnotic response is the increased motivation elicited by the demand characteristics associated with hypnotic techniques [51]. Participants are more highly motivated to engage in the therapist's requests while in the hypnotic state. Enhancing participants' motivation may be beneficial to a degree; it could be suggested that by addressing the unconscious mind, the process of hypnosis establishes positive cognitions that are then acted upon in the conscious state. This process of communication results in positive imaging, memory recall and suggestions for future stressful idiographic encounters (tools used in hypnotherapy). Muscle relaxation and focused breathing used in the hypnotic induction contribute to the reduction of anxiety.

4.2 The rationale for integration

The rationale for the integration of the two disciplines is given below:

- Hypnosis provides a broad range of techniques that can easily be integrated into CBT. This allows CBT therapists to continue practising within the framework of their training without losing the benefits of effective techniques generated from the area of clinical hypnosis. A review of the strengths and weaknesses of CBT concluded that CBT and hypnotherapy can be combined to form a powerful treatment approach [29].

- The application of a model of cognitive hypnotherapy for various emotional problems and disorders offers a template for the guidance of future therapies and treatment strategies [29].

- The powerful treatment approach gives a quicker resolution of the unwanted condition. Rapid changes are attributed to the brisk and profound behavioural, emotional, cognitive and physiological changes brought on by hypnosis [17].

- The integrative approach offers a much needed theoretical framework, thus guiding practice [49].
- Treatment based on individual case formulation is prescriptive and not haphazard [29].

Having considered the rationale for integration of hypnosis with CBT, the next section provides a short overview of key findings from research of cognitive hypnotherapy treatments.

5. Cognitive hypnotherapy (CH): treatments

A meta-analysis was conducted by critically reviewing 18 studies where a cognitive-behavioural therapy was compared with the same therapy supplemented by hypnosis across a wide variety of targeted disorders. Evidence showed that the addition of hypnosis to CBT enhanced treatment outcome compared to CBT treatment alone. The mean scores of the patients receiving cognitive-behavioural hypnotherapy showed a substantial improvement compared with 70% of the patients receiving only CBT [52].

The use of CBT and hypnotic techniques to enhance treatment effects has occurred in various domains and several studies have demonstrated the effectiveness of the integration.

In the first controlled treatment study using hypnosis as an adjunct to CBT for acute stress, it was found that CBT + hypnosis resulted in a greater reduction in stress than CBT alone, which was still evident at a 6-month follow-up. However, the researchers reported that a limitation of the study was the lack of specific guidelines regarding the mechanisms that potentially mediate hypnosis in the context of CBT and this could have weakened the procedure as the guidelines were unclear [9].

Evidence for the added effect of combining hypnosis with CBT in the management of chronic depression was provided in a seminal investigation [29]. It was found that hypnosis enhanced the overall beneficial effect of the treatment and reduced the number of sessions needed in comparison with CBT treatment alone. This investigation using cognitive hypnotherapy met the criteria laid down by the American Association Task Force and provided validation (for patients' safety) of the integration of hypnosis with CBT in the management of depression [53]. Further information was supplied when evidence-based hypnotherapy was reviewed for the treatment of depression [8].

The potential benefits of hypnotherapy were investigated with 32 patients suffering from chronic combat-related post-traumatic stress disorder (PTSD) [54]. The patients were already being treated with anti-depressants and supportive psychotherapy and were randomised into two groups. Fifteen patients in the first group received Zolpidem 10 milligrams nightly for 14 nights, and 17 patients in the hypnotherapy group were treated by symptom-orientated hypnotherapy, two 1.5-hour sessions each week for 2 weeks. All patients completed the Stanford Hypnotic Susceptibility Scale, Beck Depression Inventory, Impact of Event Scale and Sleep Quality Questionnaire prior to and post-treatment. It was found that there was a significant main effect of condition in the hypnotherapy group on PTSD symptoms as measured on the Post-traumatic Disorder Scale, and this effect was maintained at a 1-month follow-up. No such effects were reported in the non-hypnotherapy group either during the main data collection period or at the 1-month monitoring. The hypnotherapy group experienced additional benefits: decreases in intrusion and avoidance reactions and improvement in all sleep variables assessed. This investigation demonstrates the beneficial effect of hypnotherapy with positive results achieved in a 2-week period. The methodology is robust as it uses a number of different scales and incorporates a control group. To aid further research in this domain, guidelines and protocols for the integration of hypnosis with CBT in the treatment of PTSD was set up [22].

An investigation into the treatment of headaches and migraines provided an update of the literature first reviewed in 1996 by the National Institute of Health Technology Assessment Panel on the Integration of Behavioural and Relaxation Approaches into the treatment of chronic pain and headaches. It concluded that hypnosis is very effective and virtually free of side effects and adverse reactions and it meets the clinical psychology research criteria for being a well-established treatment. The research further drew attention to the ongoing expense associated with medication treatments [55].

The literature also gives evidence of the beneficial effects of cognitive hypnotherapy in the following domains:

CH was adopted as a therapy for investigations studying irritable-bowel syndrome-induced agoraphobia [56]. The research demonstrated the efficacy of CBT with the integration of hypnosis, and the effectiveness of this multi-modal treatment in aiding the accompanying agoraphobia. A further study into irritable bowel syndrome condition using hypnotic techniques was conducted with eight female patients [57]. This research supported the earlier findings and demonstrated a significant improvement in the quality of life of the patients.

Hypnotic techniques have also been researched regarding common sleep disorders [58]. However, there appears to be little empirical 'sleep research' integrating CBT with hypnosis. Therefore, the goal of this research was to educate clinicians on how to incorporate hypnosis with CBT in the management of sleep disturbance. This will be of value both in this research field and to therapists.

Hypnosis as an adjunct to therapy has been investigated in the management of both Type 1 and Type 2 diabetes [59]. The authors report that hypnotherapy appears to be psychologically beneficial and warrants further investigations. The findings indicate promising results for the stabilisation of blood glucose and decreased peripheral vascular complications. However, it is not reported whether comparisons were made with a control group, where no treatment was given, which would be a limitation of this research. It has been argued as to what constitutes sound methodology [54]; the minimal threshold of 'soundness' suggested is a design that compares a treatment with some form of minimal or non-treatment condition. The above investigation into diabetes however adds to current knowledge and is important in highlighting the effects that psychological aspects exert on recovery of this condition.

Hypnotherapy studies have been conducted in the following domains: pain management in burn patients [60], pain relief during labour and childbirth [61] and mild hypertension [62]. The results of these studies indicate that the psychological treatment through hypnotherapy can be very beneficial; however, the studies appear not to have a control group, which weakens the research.

Investigations have also been conducted in performance anxiety using hypnosis as an adjunct to therapy.

Performance anxiety and treatment outcome were investigated when CBT and CBT with hypnosis were tested for effective treatment of public speaking anxiety. It was found that although both treatments effectively reduced anxiety when performing, the addition of hypnosis to CBT generated expectancies for greater change among participants, which further enhanced treatment effects and produced a faster drop in anxiety levels post-treatment [63]. It was concluded in a review of the empirical status of the use of hypnosis in conjunction with CBT programmes [64] that existing studies demonstrate substantial benefits by the use of hypnosis as an adjunct to CBT, supporting the meta-analysis conducted in 1995 [52].

A large-scale study was conducted with pianists looking at the effect of hypnotherapy on music performance anxiety (MPA) [65]. Using two groups, it was found that the hypnotherapy group but not the control group showed a significant reduction in MPA post-intervention, which was still evident 6 months later. At that time, there were no definitive protocols and procedure for the adoption of CH as an intervention for MPA but these have now been recently documented, giving guidelines and clear directives for the process of integration in this domain [47].

Recent research was conducted into MPA with 46 advanced pianists where participants were randomly assigned to a cognitive hypnotherapy (CH), eye movement desensitisation and reprocessing (EMDR) or non-treatment group and given two sessions only of the allocated therapy. They were tested in two concert performances pre- and post-intervention. Significant decreases in performance anxiety (the cognitive, physiological and behavioural aspects of performance) were found in both the therapy groups but not in the control group [66]. This research was extended when trait levels of anxiety (an individual's general anxiety level) were tested at 4 months and 1 year post-intervention. Statistical evidence at both monitoring points demonstrated a significant reduction in trait anxiety levels below baseline, showing the effectiveness of both CH and EMDR over time [67].

Nine case studies documenting performance anxiety in different domains have recently been published (five in music, two in the sports arena and two in the workplace) where CH was one of the interventions adopted. The effects of CH were recorded immediately post-intervention and longitudinally, and shown to be beneficial in a short space of time for the reduction of negative, psychological perceptions in a performing situation [68].

The findings from the above studies indicate that the addition of hypnosis to CBT protocols for the treatment of a variety of disorders is an effective remedy. It brings positive change rapidly in cognitive perceptions and physiology which impacts on subjective behaviour. However, there appear to be few guidelines for an integrative procedure and the assimilation of hypnotic techniques for the treatment of diverse medical conditions, and this needs to be addressed in future research.

As hypnosis influences behavioural and psychological responses, it is difficult to assess whether a placebo effect is operative here and, if it is, the extent to which it plays a role. For a number of individuals, hypnosis may act as a placebo due to positive expectations. There is evidence that hypnotic trance inductions are beneficial for those patients who believe in their efficacy [13, 69] and there is further evidence that patients' attitudes and beliefs can have a profound therapeutic effect on both medical and psychological conditions [70]. This effect may be difficult or impossible to control but if it enhances suggestibility and positive therapeutic outcome, then it can be beneficial and add to the impact and strength of the therapy.

6. Conclusion

This chapter has reviewed the evidence and given the rationale for the assimilation of hypnotic techniques with CBT and has documented the effects of CH treatments in a number of different domains. There is a growing body of scientific literature attesting to the fact that hypnosis enhances CBT, and a plethora of research suggesting that combining CBT with hypnosis is effective for a variety of psychological, behavioural and medical disorders. It has been shown that the addition of hypnosis shortens the number of sessions required to effect beneficial, rapid change, which is long-lasting. One-dimensional procedures have their limitations; however, a multi-modal approach integrating hypnosis and CBT offers an effective alternative. A weakness of CBT therapies is the number of sessions required and there appears to be a paucity of research in the general domain using comparative interventions of CBT with CH [9, 52, 63]. This needs to be addressed in future studies so that comparisons of symptom effects and number of therapy sessions required can be assessed. There is case formulation, including guidelines and protocols, in the domains of PTSD, the management of depression and in music performance anxiety. However, there appears to be little empirical research with case formulation pertaining to the use of CH for the treatment of diverse medical conditions or the management of anxiety per se. An assimilative integrative model that can be understood and undertaken by therapists in the field is required. This will increase and verify the credibility of CH and help both scientific researchers and clinical therapists have a greater understanding of this psychodynamic therapy.

Author details

Elizabeth Brooker
University of Leeds, Leeds, UK

*Address all correspondence to: elizabeth.brooker@hotmail.co.uk

References

[1] Alladin A. Cognitive hypnotherapy with depression. Journal of Cognitive Psychotherapy: An International Quarterly. 1994;**8**(4):275-288

[2] Barnett EA. Analytical Hypnotherapy: Principles and Practice. Glendale, CA: Westwood Publishing; 1989

[3] Tebbetts C. Self-Hypnosis and Other Mind–Expanding Techniques. Glendale, CA: Westwood Publishing Company; 1987

[4] Rossi EL, Cheek DB. Mind-Body Therapy: Methods of Ideodynamic Healing in Hypnosis. New York: W. W. Norton; 1994

[5] Kazdin AE. Integration of psychodynamic and behavioural psychotherapies: Conceptual versus empirical synthesis. In: Arkowitz H, Messer SB, editors. Psychoanalytic Therapy and Behavior Therapy: Is Integration Possible? New York: Plenum; 1984. pp. 139-170

[6] Nathanson DL. Affect and hypnosis: On paying friendly attention to disturbing thoughts. International Journal of Clinical and Experimental Hypnosis. 2009;**57**(4):319-342

[7] Appel SS. Modifying solo performance anxiety in adult pianists. Journal of Music Therapy. 1976;**13**(1):2-16

[8] Alladin A. Evidence-based hypnotherapy for depression. International Journal of Clinical and Experimental Hypnosis. 2010;**58**(2):165-185

[9] Bryant R, Moulds ML, Guthrie R, Nixon R. The additive benefit of hypnosis and cognitive-behavioral therapy in treating acute stress disorder. Journal of Consulting and Clinical Psychology. 2005;**73**:334-340

[10] Dozois DJA, Westra HA. The nature of anxiety and depression: Implications for prevention. In: Dozois DJA, Dobson KS, editors. The Prevention of Anxiety and Depression: Theory, Research, and Practice. Washington, DC: American Psychological Association; 2004. pp. 9-41

[11] Spiegel D, Classen C. Acute stress disorder. In: Gabbard GO, editor. Treatments of Psychiatric Disorders. Vol. 2. Washington, DC: American Psychiatric Publishing; 1995. pp. 1521-1535

[12] Brown DP, Fromm E. Hypnotherapy and Behavioral Medicine. Hillsdale, NJ: Lawrence Erlbaum; 1986b

[13] Lazarus AA. 'Hypnosis' as a facilitator in behaviour therapy. International Journal of Clinical and Experimental Hypnosis. 1973;**6**:83-89

[14] Bandura A. Self-efficacy: Toward a unifying theory of behavioral change. Psychological Review. 1977;**84**(2):191-215

[15] Dengrove E. The use of hypnosis in behaviour therapy. International Journal of Clinical and Experimental Hypnosis. 1973;**21**:13-17

[16] Yapko MD. Trancework: An Introduction to the Practice of Clinical Hypnosis. 3rd ed. New York: Brunner-Routledge; 2003

[17] DePiano FA, Salzberg HC, editors. Clinical Applications of Hypnosis. Norwood, NJ: Ablex; 1986

[18] Erickson MH, Rossi E. Hypnotherapy: An Exploratory Casebook. New York: Irvington; 1979

[19] Brown DP, Fromm E. Hypnotherapy and Hypnoanalysis. Hillsdale, NJ: Lawrence Erlbaum; 1986a

[20] Erickson MH, Rossi E. Varieties of hypnotic amnesia. American Journal of Clinical Hypnosis. 1974;**17**:143-157

[21] Heap M, Aravind KK. Hartland's Medical and Dental Hypnosis. 4th ed. Churchill: Livingstone; 2002

[22] Alladin A. Cognitive Hypnotherapy: An Integrated Approach to the Treatment of Emotional Disorders. Chichester, West Sussex: John Wiley & Sons; 2008

[23] Tosi DJ, Baisden BS. Cognitive-experiential therapy and hypnosis. In: Wester WC, Smith AH, editors. Clinical Hypnosis: A Multidisciplinary Approach. Philadelphia: J.B. Lippincott; 1984. pp. 155-178

[24] Pribram K. Languages of the Brain: Experimental Paradoxes and Principles in Neuro-Psychology. 3rd ed. New York: Brandon House; 1971

[25] Pribram K. The cognitive revolution and mind/brain issues. American Psychologist. 1986;**41**(5):507-520

[26] Boutin G. The treatment of test anxiety by rational stage directed hypnotherapy. American Journal of Clinical Hypnosis. 1978;**21**:52

[27] Ley RG, Freeman RJ. Imagery, cerebral laterality, and the healing process. In: Sheikh AA, editor. Imagination and Healing. New York: Baywood; 1984. pp. 51-68

[28] Barrios AA. Posthypnotic suggestion in high-order conditioning: A methodological and experimental analysis. International Journal of Clinical and Experimental Hypnosis. 1973;**21**:32-50

[29] Alladin A, Alibhai A. Cognitive-hypnotherapy for depression: An empirical investigation. International Journal of Clinical and Experimental Hypnosis. 2007;**55**:147-166

[30] Lyubomirsky S, Tkach C. The consequences of dysphoric rumination. In: Papageorgiou C, Wells A, editors. Depressive Rumination: Nature Theory and Treatment. Chichester: John Wiley & Sons; 2004. pp. 21-41

[31] Beck AT. Thinking and depression. Part II: Theory and therapy. Archives of General Psychiatry. 1964;**9**:324-333

[32] Baddeley AD. Essentials of Human Memory. Hove: Psychology Press; 1999

[33] Wells NA, Hahn BA, Whorell PJ. Clinical economics review: Irritable bowel syndrome. Alimentary Pharmacology & Therapeutics. 1997;**11**: 1019-1030

[34] Wells A. Cognitive therapy case formulation in anxiety disorders. In: Tarrier N, editor. Case Formulation in Cognitive Behaviour Therapy. Hove, UK: Routledge; 2006. pp. 52-80

[35] Watson JB. Psychology from the Standpoint of a Behaviourist. Philadelphia: Lippincott; 1924

[36] Skinner BF. Science and Human Behaviour. New York, NY: Macmillan; 1953

[37] Wolfe BE. Understanding and Treating Anxiety Disorders: An Integrative Approach to Healing the Wounded Self. Washington: American Psychological Association; 2005

[38] Wills F. Beck's Cognitive Therapy. Hove: Routledge; 2009

[39] Beck AT. Cognitive therapy: Nature and relation to behaviour therapy. Behavior Therapy. 1970;**1**(2):184-200

[40] Wolpe J, Lazarus AA. Behavior Therapy Techniques: A Guide to the Treatment of Neuroses. New York: Pergamon Press; 1966

[41] Brewin CR. Theoretical foundations of cognitive behaviour therapy for anxiety and depression. Annual Review of Psychology. 1996;**47**:33-57

[42] Cooper P. Introduction: Why cognitive behavior therapy? In: Butler G, editor. Overcoming Social Anxiety and Shyness. London: Robinson Publishing; 1999

[43] Kenny DT, Osborne MS. Music performance anxiety: New insights from young musicians. Advances in Cognitive Psychology. 2006;**2**(2-3):103-112

[44] Butler G. Overcoming Social Anxiety and Shyness. London: Robinson Publishing; 1999

[45] Persons JB. Cognitive Therapy: A Case Formulation Approach. New York: W. W. Norton; 1989

[46] Clark A. Supersizing the Mind: Embodiment, Action, and Cognitive Extension. New York, NY: Oxford University Press; 2008

[47] Brooker E. Music Performance Anxiety: An Investigation into the Efficacy of Cognitive Hypnotherapy and Eye Movement Desensitisation and Reprocessing when applied to Grade 8 Pianists [Doctoral dissertation thesis]. UK: University of Leeds. 2015. Available from: http://etheses.whiterose.ac.uk/12130

[48] Golden WL. Cognitive-behavioral hypnotherapy for anxiety disorders. Journal of Cognitive Hypnotherapy. 1994;**8**:265-274

[49] Messer S. A critical examination of belief structures in integrative and eclectic psychotherapy. In: Norcross JC, Goldfried MR, editors. Handbook of Psychotherapy Integration. New York: Basic Books; 1992. pp. 130-168

[50] Blenkiron P. Stories and analogies in cognitive behaviour therapy: A clinical review. Behavioural and Cognitive Psychotherapy. 2005;**33**:45-59

[51] Spanos NP. Hypnotic behaviour: A social-psychological interpretation of amnesia, analgesia, and "trance logic". Behavioral and Brain Sciences. 1986;**9**:449-467

[52] Kirsch I, Montgomery G, Saperstein G. Hypnosis as an adjunct to cognitive-behavioral psychotherapy: A meta-analysis. Journal of Consulting and Clinical Psychology. 1995;**63**:214-220

[53] Chambless DL, Hollon SD. Defining empirically supported therapies. Journal of Consulting and Clinical Psychology. 1998;**66**:7-18

[54] Abramowitz EG, Barak Y, Ben-Avi I, Knobler HY. Hypnotherapy in the treatment of chronic combat-related PTSD patients suffering from insomnia: A randomised, Zolpidem-controlled clinical trial. International Journal of Clinical and Experimental Hypnosis. 2008;**56**(3):270-280

[55] Hammond DC. Review of the efficacy of clinical hypnosis with headaches and migraines. International Journal of Clinical and Experimental Hypnosis. 2007;**55**:207-219

[56] Golden WL. Cognitive-behavioral hypnotherapy in the treatment of irritable-bowel syndrome-induced agoraphobia. International Journal of Clinical and Experimental Hypnosis. 2007;**55**(2):131-146

[57] Keefer L, Keshavarzian A. Feasibility and acceptability of gut-directed hypnosis on inflammatory bowel disease: A brief communication. International Journal of Clinical and Experimental Hypnosis. 2007;**55**(4):457-466

[58] Graci GM, Hardie JC. Evidence-based hypnotherapy for the

management of sleep disorders. International Journal of Clinical and Experimental Hypnosis. 2007;**55**:288-302

[59] Xu Y, Cardena E. Hypnosis as an adjunct therapy in the management of diabetes. International Journal of Clinical and Experimental Hypnosis. 2008;**56**(1):63-92

[60] Shakibaei F, Harandi AA, Gholamrezaei A, Samoei R, Salehi P. Hypnotherapy in management of pain and re-experiencing of trauma in burn patients. International Journal of Clinical and Experimental Hypnosis. 2008;**56**(2):185-197

[61] Abbasi M, Ghazi F, Barlow-Harrison A, Sheikhvatan M, Mohammadyan F. The effect of hypnosis on pain relief during labor and childbirth in Iranian pregnant women. International Journal of Clinical and Experimental Hypnosis. 2009;**57**(2):174-183

[62] Gay M-C. Effectiveness of hypnosis in reducing mild essential hypertension: A one-year follow-up. International Journal of Clinical and Experimental Hypnosis. 2007;**55**(1):67-83

[63] Schoenberger NE, Kirsch I, Gearan P, Montgomery G, Pastyrmak S. Hypnotic enhancement of a cognitive-behavioral treatment for public speaking anxiety. Behavior Therapy. 1997;**28**:127-140

[64] Schoenberger NE. Research on hypnosis as an adjunct to cognitive-behavioral psychotherapy. International Journal of Clinical and Experimental Hypnosis. 2000;**48**:154-169

[65] Stanton HE. Reduction of performance anxiety in music students. Australian Psychologist. 1994;**29**(2):124-127

[66] Brooker E. Music performance anxiety: A clinical outcome study into the effects of cognitive hypnotherapy and eye movement desensitisation and reprocessing in advanced pianists. Psychology of Music. 2018;**46**(1):107-124

[67] Brooker E. Cognitive hypnotherapy and EMDR: The longitudinal effects on trait anxiety and music performance in advanced pianists. Advances in Complementary & Alternative medicine. 2019;**5**(4):ACAM.000616.2019

[68] Brooker E. Transforming Performance Anxiety Treatment Using Cognitive Hypnotherapy and EMDR. London and New York: Routledge; 2019

[69] Spanos NP, Barber TX. Toward a convergence in hypnosis research. American Psychologist. 1974;**29**:500-511

[70] Harrington A, editor. The Placebo Effect. Cambridge, MA. Harvard University Press; 1997

Chapter 6

Active-Alert Hypnosis to Achieve Personal, Professional, and Therapeutic Goals

Arnoldo Téllez, Arturo Valdez and Teresa Sánchez-Jáuregui

Abstract

Hypnosis does not always require suggestions of relaxation in order enter into this state. It can also be induced through suggestions of activation and cognitive alertness. This procedure and the hypnotic state caused by it has been called active-alert hypnosis (AAH). In this chapter, we describe a strategy to increase the probability to achieve goals using an AAH technique in which we ask the patient to move his arms in an alternate way, while imagining that he has a pair of dumbbells of several kilograms in each hand, in order to produce a hypnotic age progression phenomenon, in which the patient is oriented to a positive future and mobilizing hope, and could see himself achieving his goals, creating "memories of the future." We report several clinical cases in which this hypnotic strategy was used.

Keywords: active-alert hypnosis, goals achievement, age progression, prospective memory

1. Just a little background on hypnosis and hypnotherapy

Over time, hypnosis has been defined in various ways. In its early stages, it was associated with supernatural states. The current official definition, according to the American Psychological Association, is "a state of consciousness, involving a focused attention and reduced peripheral awareness, characterized by an enhanced capacity for response to suggestions" [1]. Unestahl [2] defines hypnosis as "an alternative state of consciousness, where information can bypass the logical mind and bring about changes in suggestibility and perception and in which there are alternative control systems available." Taking both definitions into account, we propose the following definition that describes this state of consciousness more broadly:

> *Hypnosis is a state of intense and focused attention that leads us to a special state of consciousness, in which previously learned experiences can be evoked in an involuntary way. This state is characterized by an increase in suggestibility and the ability to modify the perception, memory, and functioning of the autonomic nervous system [3].*

In the past, it was also common knowledge that hypnosis implies a relaxation, or a sleep-like state, in which the hypnotized person loses his/her consciousness temporarily, being completely under the hypnotist's control. Now, however, it is known that hypnosis is a natural state that tends to occur periodically several times a day, approximately every 90 min in human beings, as one of many psychobiological ultradian rhythms [4] during which the person is in total control of his/her will [5].

According to our definition of hypnosis, we can say that this state is not limited to a relaxed state but any state of focused attention that switches our mind to a more creative mode, helping us to find solutions for specific problems or seeing things from a different perspective, enhancing the capacity to access unconscious memories and perceptions and to reframe them, and facilitating processes of dissociation.

2. Active-alert hypnosis: a path to our goals

In her 1973 doctoral dissertation, Eva Banyai explained her study about the effects of hypnosis in verbal learning that involved 24 patients. She stated that the majority of subjects achieved a classic hypnotic state (a relaxed, passive state), but four of them exhibited a different state:

> *... four subjects exhibited a different behavior: They were in an even "more active" state than the waking ones. They followed the instructions of the experimenter immediately, while their fast movements, lively facial expressions, loud voices, and their fast speech were in sharp contrast with the passive behavior of the average subjects. It was as if they had been released from some kind of pressure, their behavior reflected childlike playfulness [6].*

That unexpected finding suggested that hypnosis is not only a relaxed state, but is also a wide spectrum of "altered" conscious states that can be subjectiveley experienced in many different forms by each individual with different behavioral and physiological outcomes.

Banyai called this kind of hypnotic state "active-alert hypnosis." She also stated that the sleep-like outcomes in traditional hypnosis occur due to suggestions from the facilitator rather than from the hypnosis itself. This modality of hypnosis has been applied to high-performing athletes with significantly positive results [1], but also with people who prefer an eyes-open trance, or a more active one. In our experience, this type of induction can also be used for visualization and reaching one's own personal and professional goals.

The original active alert-hypnosis approaches were performed while pedaling a stationary bicycle, receiving hypnotic suggestions of activation and alertness, paying attention to the feelings in their legs, to automatic movement, to their energy, and to their inner peace [7, 8].

According to Banyai [6], active-alert hypnosis has been a useful tool in the following cases:

- Lack of initiative and energy
- General inhibition
- Excessively withdrawn personality
- Depression
- Anxiety disorders
- Inhibited identity development

- Eating disorders (bulimia and obesity)
- Children who do not tolerate the stillness of traditional hypnosis
- Enhancement of physical and mental performance in healthy people (including competitive athletes)

Since these original approaches were performed, several methods of achieving an active-alert hypnotic state have been developed. For example, Etzel Cardeña [9] elaborated a gentle active-alert hypnotic technique consisting of simply waving one hand up and down, producing results similar to those of Banyai's study. Even though active-alert hypnotic approaches are used primarily in therapeutic contexts, you can also notice "altered" consciousness states and active-alert hypnotic states in other contexts, such as religious ceremonies, highly competitive sports (while practicing or watching), dancing, teaching, writing, playing a musical instrument, and many other activities that require highly focused attention. This kind of hypnosis has been called in different ways: hyper-alert hypnosis, active hypnosis, waking hypnosis, awake-alert hypnosis, and alert hypnosis.

3. Goals and motivation

I (AV) would like to share an experience I had some time ago. A friend of mine asked me to slightly change my way of dressing to become a more presentable professional, to give a different image to others and to myself. I have to admit that a part of me was reluctant to make that change, while the other one was just a little curious about what could change for the better if I follow his advice. That curiosity led me to a little inspection of my closet, with some dirty and old clothes hanging there along with some clothes that I did not really use, but there they were, and I came to realize that I needed to go get new clothes, and a new pair of shoes, because my old ones, although comfy, were starting to rip apart, and we all need a good pair of formal and comfortable shoes for formal occasions. After making the decision to go and buy some new clothes and a new pair of shoes, the instruction "buy a pair of shoes" was imprinted in my mind, nothing else.

Get inside the shop, with all those different kinds of shoes, selecting just one pair of them was a difficult task. But my mind was clear: "buy a pair of shoes." I bought a brown pair of shoes, and they were going to be worn next Monday. That day, I put them on and walked a little, and after a few blocks my ankle started to hurt. It was a weak but annoying pain. After a few more blocks, the skin of my Achilles tendon started to peel and I felt an even more annoying pain, and I remembered thinking, "But these shoes are new. Why is this happening?"

Now when we make plans, we not only use our conscious mind, but we also use our unconscious one [10]. The question here is: how?

According to some research [11, 12], our brain makes decisions even before we think we made them. Let us explain this statement. Imagine that we suggest that you move your lips to the right when you see something beautiful and to your left when you see something that you think is not. Then I show you some images on a screen. When you see an image, the information travels all the way through your visual processing structures in your brain (occipital lobe structures), then after being analyzed it is sent to an interpretation area (temporo-parieto-occipital region), and then to our decision-making structures (prefrontal region) to decide whether it is beautiful. That takes no more than a few microseconds, but it is a complex process, all happening without you realizing it. Now that you have decided to make the movement to the left or right, your frontal lobe sends a signal to your lips to "move" left or right. That is when it gets tricky: it appears that your brain sends that last signal *before* your prefrontal region does its job.

Can we say that our decision-making process and motivation are, therefore, unconscious? If so, how can we develop a stronger will and motivation to make different or even better decisions? Some evidence suggests that the decision-making process comes from a mixture of conscious and unconscious mind [13].

As hypnotherapists, we are accustomed to "talking to the unconscious mind" [14] and that includes avoiding some of the intellectual and logical barriers that one builds for oneself. In hypnosis, that is achieved through hypnotic suggestions. Weitzenhoffer [15, 16] claims that the difference between a hypnotic suggestion and an order is the nonvolitional outcome after the hypnotic suggestion, that is, the hypnotized person does not act according to conscious will but rather in a "dissociative" mode: "it's as if the levitating arm were not mine." As Farvolden and Woody [17] find on their study, diminished activity on frontal lobe structures could be an explanation to this "unconscious" behavior. And that is the key aspect of a hypnotic and posthypnotic suggestions, the nonconscious willingness.

Now, how can we use this process to achieve goals? That is what we will be exploring in this chapter.

4. Prospective memory

"It's a poor sort of memory that only works backwards."

Lewis Carroll (Alice in Wonderland).

Prospective memory is the ability that allows us to make plans in the present and then remember and carry them out in the future [18]. It is known that the hippocampus consolidates memory from short term to long term [19] and such a complex process occurs better while sleeping [20]. Also, the amygdala's involvement in the memory consolidation process is well demonstrated since a memory associated with high-intensity emotional content tends to last longer than a boring one [21, 22].

In the prefrontal cortex, the Brodmann area 10 seems to be responsible for making plans and translating them into action, with support from the structures mentioned above. Also, the same area is responsible for retrieving information about those plans and maintaining the attention required to execute them [23].

5. How to use hypnosis to facilitate prospective memory

As Milton Erickson said

> *There has to be an integration of unconscious learnings with conscious learnings. This should be foremost in your mind whenever you use hypnosis on psychiatric patients. You can recognize that you can resolve a conflict, a phobia, or an anxiety in the trance state. But unless you do something about it in the waking state, the patient is still likely to have that anxiety or phobia. ([14], p. 6)*

There are some classic hypnotic phenomena reported in literature, such as:

- Amnesia-hypermnesia
- Catalepsy
- Analgesia

- Age regression
- Hypnotic hallucination
- Posthypnotic suggestion
- Automatic writing
- Age progression
- Hypnotic age progression

We will focus on hypnotic age progression in this section. Age progression is a procedure that projects the person *into* the future to experience achieving her/his goals as if they were happening right now [24]. This involves not only seeing them as a dissociated image, but also as an associated one, where you can see exactly what you will be seeing, and feeling what you will be feeling once you have accomplished an objective, and then be aware of the steps you take to reach that goal, as if they were made in the past. This approach was used by Erickson in many forms, including the "crystal ball" hypnotic strategy.

Now, when you work with this pseudo-orientation in time, you need to make contact with the conscious mind, and that is where goal construction takes place.

According to Robert Dilts [25], people construct their goals using six principal methods:

- negation of the problematic state
- defining the goal as the polarity or the opposite of the problematic state
- using an external role model or reference to define the desired state
- taking some key characteristics of the desired state
- making a generative outcome (using their own references instead of external ones)
- acting "as if"

When you are working to generate changes with people, all psychotherapy approaches usually take time to define goals. Some methods establish them in a positive and a future-oriented way, for example "What you are going to be doing once you feel..." [26], or focused on what is going to be happening once you get rid of your problem [27]. In our experience, people often struggle with the construction of their objective because they are ambiguous and lacking both clarity and a deadline. Also people focus on what they do not want rather than on what they really want to reach or accomplish.

6. Active-alert hypnosis for goal achievement

Now, we are presenting an active-alert hypnotic strategy to increase motivation and visualize goals, a methodology that has shown excellent results in our practice, and that currently is being tested for efficacy not only in therapeutic contexts but also through the use of scientific methodology.

6.1 First step: writing your goals

In our experience, the approach that has been most useful in helping people to formulate their goals consists of four simple rules:

- Write your goal in the first person: Always start with "I...," even if it is obvious that the goal refers to you, it is important to express it with certainty.
- Write your goal in the present or in the present progressive tense: Use "I'm" and "I'm being" instead of using the future tense.
- Describe your goal with as many details as possible: Remember that if you give details to them, some goals could seem smaller and therefore more attainable.
- Write your goals in a positive way: For example, instead of thinking, "I do not want to get sick," you should write, "I am a healthy person."

Here is an example. A common goal is "I want to lose weight." Now, following those four rules, we can formulate that goal in this way:

> *I am (first person, and present tense) a healthy person, I have a waist measuring 70 centimeters, and I weigh 60 kg. (Written in a positive sentence), I am eating the healthy food that my nutritionist has suggested, and I drink at least two liters of water each day. I exercise five days per week: I do a gym workout and lift weights on three days and on the other two days I do cardio sessions (providing as many details as possible).*

We ask the person to write two or three goals for every important aspect of his/her life. Then we ask them to read these goals out loud while imagining him/herself in that moment, reaching that goal.

6.2 Second step: overcoming fears and limitations

In this second part of the exercise, we ask the patient to write a different list following these instructions:

> *All those things that you thought have stopped you from reaching your goals, all those silly things that you said to yourself that made you feel like you might not be able to reach them... maybe all those fears that you had before and that stopped you from success until now.*

In my experience (AT), fear is the principal enemy of setting and achieving your goals, but optimism and good self-esteem will also act as your allies all the way to success.

> *All those fears and limitations are just like a malicious software, like a computer virus... more like trash... like garbage... like waste... mental trash or mental waste or mental garbage that maybe were put there by somebody that wasn't you, maybe with or without intention... but you can get rid of this trash... of this malicious mental software... you can throw away that waste... you can throw away that garbage.*

Once all of these fears and limitations are written on a sheet of paper, we tell the person to say goodbye to them, and tear up the paper with all her/his strength. We tell them:

Now that those fears are in that paper... that garbage is in that list... I want you to rip apart that mental waste... with all your strength... to tear that sheet of paper into small... unrecognizable pieces... that cannot be put together again... very small... unrecognizable... insignificant pieces... torn apart...

Now... with all your strength... throw that garbage away... mental garbage... mental trash... mental waste... should be in the place where it belongs from now on... (we bring a trash can to them) ... in this trash can... where those very small... unrecognizable... insignificant pieces of paper will be placed from now on...

(Now with louder voice) While you throw them away... those very small... unrecognizable... insignificant pieces of paper... give them a last goodbye... yell to them ... while throwing them away... ¡THAT'S RIGHT!

6.3 Third step: active-alert hypnosis facilitation: the dumbbells technique (Arnoldo Téllez, n.d.)

This is an active-alert hypnotic technique developed a few years ago, in which we ask the person to sit comfortably and look at any point (you can use a point on the wall or an image). Next, we start to suggest:

When you are ready to begin, please just sit and make yourself comfortable. Shall we start? Ok, look at that picture[1]*... I would like you to focus your attention on any point of the picture, whichever you want... Now... please put your hands with your palms facing up resting on your legs... that's right... keep looking at the same point... while you concentrate on your breath... Now... I wonder what sensations are going to emerge within your body... when you start to practice this exercise... we are going to practice an exercise ... Now... have you ever felt the sensation of a weight in your hands?... that's right... as if you have some weights in your hands right now... I want you to imagine as if you have some weights in each one of your hands, a pair of dumbbells... one in each hand... about 2 or 3 kilos... is that okay?... Right... Now... You can grab them hard... and feel the weight... 2 or 3 kilos in each hand... Right now... you do not know yet... exactly how you feel... but as you move your dumbbells up and down ... they will feel heavier... While you watch that point... start raising one dumbbell ... up to your shoulder ... Now slowly lower it... While lowing it, raise the other dumbbell... Okay... now move up and down the other one... the left arm and then the other... Right... arm... while still looking at that point... that's right ... I want you to continue looking at the same point... Maybe now you can feel how the muscles contract and then relax... I want you to feel the weight of those dumbbells... feel how the biceps, the muscles of the arms get tensed... little by little feeling warm... the energy and calories in your arms are burning... the muscles get tensed and then relaxed ... and please keep your eyes open looking at the picture... looking at the same point ... and with each movement... each time closer to know how you will be feeling... once you start moving... active... and relaxed... you become more actively relaxed... still focusing on your breathing... now take two or three deep breaths... That's right... now... every time you inhale... You can feel more and more awake ... more alert... feeling more active and full of energy... your mind is awakened... your mind is clear and lucid... can you feel it... now... your energy spreading throughout your body and your mind?... not too much or too little energy... just the right amount of energy that you need... you can feel a sensation in your body... that indicates that this energy is spreading throughout your body... toward your feet... through your legs... through your entire body... while you continue... your mind becomes more active... more lucid... clearer .... You feel more* *energized and in self-control... empowered... in harmony with yourself and your surroundings... looking at the same point... can you recognize the sensation emerging? ... now?... your arm movements make your mind become more lucid and clearer ... actively more awakened and relaxed ... that is it ... feel the movements of your body... how it gets stronger every time... with each movement of your arms ... your body and your mind get stronger and stronger... that's right... now... with every single movement... that energy of motivation is injected into your interior, a positive energy ... what do you know that will happen when... with each movement you repeat to yourself... "I can do it ... I can get it"... Right... now... visualize a goal... yes... that goal... that you wrote before... to accomplish... it could be a personal goal.... a professional goal... a goal related to your family, I do not know... but you do (k)now... this goal is your target now... and with each movement imagine... feel this sensation... that you move forward... towards your goal... you are approaching... centimeter by centimeter... meter by meter... towards your goal... just feel that sensation... as if you had some pulleys that move you towards... getting you closer to your target ... that's right... now ... with each movement you can tell yourself... you (k)now? ... "I can do it... I can get there," and you are slowly approaching your goal with each movement... closer and closer to your goal...* **Now... maybe you (k) now... or maybe you do not (k)now now... that sensation emerging through your entire body... do you remember now this sensation... you can keep it... within you... every time you need it... this sensation... you know... within you... every time you move... every time you smile... every time you see that goal... every time you breathe...** *moving forward with enthusiasm towards your goal... now... I wonder how do you want to be able to go a little faster... now... accelerating your arms movements... keep going towards that goal... more and more... towards that goal... and the more you are moving forward ... the more active and clearer your mind becomes... the clearer it becomes... the more you (k) now that sensation emerging... through all your body... with a lot of enthusiasm ... you can feel an optimistic... motivation... you become more self-confident... with your arms now moving by themselves ... by themselves... automatically... leaving behind any doubts that you thought you had... leaving behind everything... anything what you no longer need to carry on your shoulders... anything that was bothering you... that's right... now... knocking down the obstacles... clearing the way... looking more clearly forward.. with more light as you approach to your goal ... that's it... right.... safely.... with certainty ... yes... you can... you can go forward, approaching your target... your own goal...* **with that sensation in your body... within your... body... you keep it... you can remember this sensation... every time you need it... this sensation... every time you move... every time you smile... every time you see your goal... every time you breathe...** *every time you are using the best of your own inner resources... that's it... forward... right... now... there are people waiting for you there cheering... where your goal is... people who love you... to celebrate your success... more and more... recognizing your own personal strengths... maybe you did not know yourself... that people love whoever love yourself... but (k)now you (k)now yourself... leaving behind any burden that you do not need to carry out with you... breaking boundaries ... going beyond... reaching your goal... achieving the target... that's it ... right... excellent... wonderful... you almost done it... sure... yes... you can... do it... and... NOW!! you finally have reached your goal... you are already in it... right... great... amazing... enjoying ... And you can observe... and feel all those sensations... emotions... and thoughts... linked to the achievement of your goal... look right now... at this moment... inside you ... how do you feel?...* **do you *(k)now (k)now* how you feel?... that feeling emerging... through your entire body... within your... body... you keep it... you can remember this sensation... every time you need it... this**

> **sensation... every time you move... every time you smile... every time you see your goal... every time you breathe...** *now... I wonder... what emotions are linked to that success? ... Feel the happiness... Feel the satisfaction... What sensations spread throughout your body? Do you feel self-confidence in your whole body and your mind? Enjoy that feeling of reliance in yourself in having achieved your goal... And feel the wind of positive changes on your skin... And perhaps you can smell the powerful odor of your triumph... that's okay... decreasing the pace ... little by little more slowly that's it... right... savoring the success... that's right... excellent... very good... now... as you slow down a little the movement... you can close your eyes... for a moment... and breathe deeply... now you can rest your arms... you have reached your goal... feel it, enjoy this moment... you are in it ...it's your victory... you deserve it.... Do not you want to go a little further?... you... can you continue?... how much happier do you feel... now that... are you there?... yes... you are!... Breathe deeply... your mind is clear and lucid... active and positive... from now on...* **(k)now... maybe you (k)now... or maybe you do not (k)now (k)now... that sensation emerging through your entire body... you will remember now this sensation... you can keep it... within you... every time you need it... this sensation... you know... within you... every time you move... every time you smile... every time you see that goal... every time you breathe...** *And when I ask you to open your eyes and look at that point again, you will feel energized, active, and empowered, with all your potential... I do not know what positive changes your subconscious mind is going to carry out from now on... just moving, smiling, breathing... Very good ... Excellent ... Are you ready to come back here and now? How well do you feel?*

As you may notice, some of the words are italicized and we know that you are aware of how to use them, or maybe you can change them a little for your convenience.

6.4 Step four: the dirty rubber band (Arnoldo Téllez, n.d.)

Next, you can start another exercise. You may stay in the same place.

> *Now close your eyes again, we are going to do another imagination exercise... give me your hands (the therapist takes the patient's hands and pulls them forward with their palms facing one another, and he holds his/her hands on both wrists) ... okay... imagine that you have an elastic band that ties your wrists... and keeps them chained to each other... It is a dirty ... and ugly band... that holds your hands together... and do not let you be free... This band is built from former self-limitations... maybe inferiority complexes... or low self-esteem feelings... grudges... and negative comments... and they all were tying you up ... that were preventing you from being free and expanding your potential... Now I want you to start separating your hands... with all your strength... you are stretching the band... very well... while you force your hands to separate (the patient begins to open and separate his/her arms) ... continue to stretch with force... you are stretching the band more and more... You are about to break it... You are close... with more strength... You are almost to break free... almost... that's right... now... And puff! (Therapist takes the arms and separates them with the force) ... It burst!... correct... excellent... very good... expand your arms... expand your spirit... can you imagine that you are a bird? ... the bird you would like to be.... perhaps an eagle... or a hawk ... seagull... the bird you like to be.... now open your wings... with freedom... flying... You are finally free of what was holding you back... now you are free... on the top... flying... seeing from above a perspective never seen before... A horizon full of possibilities...*

right... very well... freely... quietly ... (pause a minute) ... Now you can lower your arms ... And when your arms reach your side and descend on your legs ... You will be totally... and freely... awake... Rested and awaken... How well are you feeling?

Next, here is some feedback from people who experienced this approach:

A 24-year-old man who suffered a chronic sense of demotivation and a lack of specific and clear goals in his life:

First part
"I visualized myself achieving every single goal that guided me towards my main goal. I pictured myself getting good grades, I felt joyful and happy, I visualized myself with my family sharing my success and my main goal achieved."

Second part
"I felt as if I was finally released from something so strong that was keeping me tied up. I felt an unbelievable sense of freedom, I felt a bunch of adrenaline, a burst of energy inside me."

"I could feel the air in my face, like I was really flying in the air, and I finally saw a big bright shining light from the sun."

Report from a patient with depression and anxiety after an active-alert hypnosis session:

First part
"I felt a huge amount of blood pumping fast up to my head and then running down to my stomach."

"I feel more relaxed and peaceful."

Second part
"I felt how the adrenaline rushes through my body from my stomach to my brain. This sensation makes me feel euphoric and generates emotion and happiness, something that I haven't felt for a long time."

"This is a feeling that I haven't experienced before, but now I only feel the energy from the front side of my brain to my mouth, and even more than the energy, I feel relaxation and inner peace."

"I don't feel exhausted, but relaxed."

7. Some general guidelines to apply active-alert hypnotic procedure

There is no big difference between how the linguistic structure is applied in common, relaxed trances, as you may have seen in the approach we share with you, there are some "hypnotic language forms" [24] or "Milton Model" patterns [28, 29], such as analogical marks, interspersal, ambiguities (phonological and punctuation), or lack of a referential index, among others.

In addition, the use of posthypnotic suggestions is key to the construction of a good and effective hypnotic script, since you are looking for a "posthypnotic behavior" [30] integrated into the "normal" behavior of the person [5], and there are some suggestions for their usage [3]:

- Say them at different times and with depth in the trance session
- Express it in different language levels (such as metaphorical, explicit, or with ambiguity)
- Express them as a contingent suggestion (the standard form is "next time that you [unavoidable fact], you will [suggestion]")
- Use distinctive nonverbal cues to indicate that suggestion's importance.

Unestahl [2] states that every time that a posthypnotic suggestion is triggered, a "posthypnotic trance" occurs, providing an opportunity for the person to elicit all the sensations and learning acquired in the hypnotic session and to bring them to a context where they will be useful.

There is a process in our brain called hippocampal offline replay that allows our memory to consolidate while in a sleep state. However, there is evidence suggesting that this process can occur in a special consciousness state (relaxed awake state) to bring back learned behaviors or sequences of thoughts in a shorter period of time [31, 32]. That process may be the one that will help us to consolidate and accomplish our most important goals through active-alert hypnosis, posthypnotic suggestions, and clearer goal setting.

This did not happen with that half-baked goal of mine about "getting some new shoes" because that instruction was not specific enough to obtain the desired result. My hippocampus just replays "new shoes... new shoes" a lot, without any more details, and that is what I obtained in the end. A better hypnotic suggestion might have been the following "buy a pair of new and *comfortable* shoes."

8. Conclusion

Active-alert hypnotic states could be an alternative in some cases where traditional, relaxed-state hypnosis may not be applied. This approach can be used as a tool to guide people to realize how hypnosis could be experienced on a daily basis and as an auto-hypnosis method, making use of posthypnotic trance states.

Reaching a goal requires people to think, to feel, and to act, both consciously and unconsciously. Both active-alert hypnosis and traditional relaxed-state hypnosis help to store goal-seeking information into the unconscious mind in order to encourage the person to reach his/her goals in a nonconscious manner. However, an advantage of active-alert hypnosis is that it seems to increase motivation and energy as well as increasing the probability of producing a state of flow.

According to our experience, this dumbbells technique is an excellent tool helping people to set and achieve their own goals, whatever they are: personal, professional, financial, and health-related ones. Also, in many cases it could produce a flow state characterized by a focused attention and full concentration, merging awareness and action, "freedom" from worries about failure, self-consciousness disappearing, distorted time sense, and auto-rewarding experiences [33]; this flow state leads the person to a higher motivation and energy, augmented self-efficiency perception, mind clarity, and self-control.

AAH could be very useful in high-performance athletes, as has been shown by Unestahl's research [30]. We have used the dumbbells technique, as a kind of AAH, in several cases of high-performance athletes and sport teams, from amateurs to professionals. The following is a report from a female cyclist who won gold medal in 2018 Pan-American games, who experienced this technique after a session of AAH dumbbells technique:

> *"I felt all the people in the stadium was screaming, encouraging me… to arrive the finish line in first place… I felt how my legs were stronger and faster as time goes by… once I reached the goal I felt proud, happiness, and a lot of inner peace."*

We invite you to develop your own approaches, keeping in mind that there are many kinds of hypnotic states and that you can elicit those states just by talking, even about something trivial, like your wardrobe, following conversational hypnotic patterns, by reading while your unconscious learns something without you noticing it yet, you know?

Conflict of interest

The authors have no conflicts of interest.

Author details

Arnoldo Téllez[1*], Arturo Valdez[2] and Teresa Sánchez-Jáuregui[2]

1 Psychology School and Health Sciences Research and Development Center (CIDICS), Autonomous University of Nuevo León, Monterrey, Mexico

2 Health Sciences Research and Development Center (CIDICS), Autonomous University of Nuevo León, Monterrey, Mexico

*Address all correspondence to: arnoldo.tellez@uanl.mx

References

[1] Elkins GR, Barabasz AF, Council JR, Spiegel D. Advancing research and practice: The revised APA division 30 definition of hypnosis. International Journal of Clinical and Experimental Hypnosis. 2015;**63**(1):1-9

[2] Unestahl LE. Alert, eyes-open sport hypnosis. American Journal of Clinical Hypnosis. 2018;**61**(2):159-172

[3] Téllez A. Hipnosis Clínica: Un Enfoque Ericksoniano. México: Trillas; 2007

[4] Rossi EL, Nimmons D. The 20-Minute Break: Reduce Stress, Maximize Performance, and Improve Health and Emotional Well-Being Using the New Science of Ultradian Rhythms. USA: JP Tarcher; 1991

[5] Yapko MD. Trancework: An Introduction to the Practice of Clinical Hypnosis. UK: Routledge; 2012

[6] Bányai ÉI. Active-alert hypnosis: History, research, and applications. American Journal of Clinical Hypnosis. 2018;**61**(2):88-107

[7] Banyai EI, Hilgard ER. A comparison of active-alert hypnotic induction with traditional relaxation induction. Journal of Abnormal Psychology. 1976;**85**(2):218

[8] Bányai ÉI, Zseni A, Túry F. Active-alert hypnosis in psychotherapy. In: Rhue JW, Lynn SJ, Kirsch I, editors. Handbook of Clinical Hypnosis American Psychological Association. 1993. p. 271-290

[9] Cardeña E, Maldonado J, Galdón MJ, Spiegel D. The hypnosis and the posttraumatic disorders. Anales De Psicología. 1999;**15**(1):147-155

[10] Custers R, Aarts H. The unconscious will: How the pursuit of goals operates outside of conscious awareness. Science. 2010;**329**(5987):47-50

[11] Libet B, Gleason CA, Wright EW, Pearl DK. Time of conscious intention to act in relation to onset of cerebral activity (readiness-potential). In: Neurophysiology of Consciousness. 1993. pp. 249-268

[12] Desmurget M, Sirigu A. A parietal-premotor network for movement intention and motor awareness. Trends in Cognitive Sciences. 2009;**13**(10):411-419

[13] Baumeister RF, Masicampo EJ, Vohs KD. Do conscious thoughts cause behavior? Annual Review of Psychology. 2011;**62**:331-361

[14] Erickson MH, Rossi EL. Experiencing Hypnosis. New York: Irvington; 1981

[15] Weitzenhoffer AM. Hypnotic susceptibility revisited. American Journal of Clinical Hypnosis. 1980;**22**(3):130-146

[16] Weitzenhoffer AM. When is an "instruction" an "instruction"? International Journal of Clinical and Experimental Hypnosis. 1974;**22**(3):258-269

[17] Farvolden P, Woody EZ. Hypnosis, memory, and frontal executive functioning. International Journal of Clinical and Experimental Hypnosis. 2004;**52**(1):3-26

[18] Hassin RR, Uleman JS, Bargh JA, editors. The New Unconscious. UK: Oxford University Press; 2004

[19] Moscovitch M, Cabeza R, Winocur G, Nadel L. Episodic memory and beyond: The hippocampus and neocortex in transformation. Annual Review of Psychology. 2016;**67**:105-134

[20] Girardeau G, Inema I, Buzsáki G. Reactivations of emotional memory in the hippocampus–amygdala system

during sleep. Nature Neuroscience. 2017;**20**(11):1634

[21] Rudebeck PH, Ripple JA, Mitz AR, Averbeck BB, Murray EA. Amygdala contributions to stimulus–reward encoding in the macaque medial and orbital frontal cortex during learning. Journal of Neuroscience. 2017;**37**(8):2186-2202

[22] Cacciaglia R, Nees F, Grimm O, Ridder S, Pohlack ST, Diener SJ, et al. Trauma exposure relates to heightened stress, altered amygdala morphology and deficient extinction learning: Implications for psychopathology. Psychoneuroendocrinology. 2017;**76**:19-28

[23] Cona G, Bisiacchi PS, Sartori G, Scarpazza C. Effects of cue focality on the neural mechanisms of prospective memory: A meta-analysis of neuroimaging studies. Scientific Reports. 2016;**6**(1):1-13

[24] Battino R, South TL. Ericksonian Approaches: A Comprehensive Manual. USA: Crown House Publishing; 2005

[25] Dilts R. From Coach to Awakener. Capitola, CA: Meta Publications; 2003

[26] De Shazer S, Dolan Y. More than Miracles: The State of the Art of Solution-Focused Brief Therapy. USA: Routledge; 2012

[27] Haley J. Problem-Solving Therapy. New York: Jossey-Bass; 1987

[28] Grinder J, DeLozier J, Bandler R. Patterns of the Hypnotic Techniques of Milton H. Erickson, MD. Vol. 2. Cupertino, CA: Meta Publications; 1975

[29] Grinder J, DeLozier J, Bandler R. Patterns of the Hypnotic Techniques of Milton H. Erickson, MD. Vol. 1. Cupertino, CA: Meta Publications; 1977

[30] Erickson MH, Rossi EL. Hypnotherapy: An Exploratory Casebook. New York: Irvington Publishers; 1979

[31] Carr MF, Jadhav SP, Frank LM. Hippocampal replay in the awake state: A potential substrate for memory consolidation and retrieval. Nature Neuroscience. 2011;**14**(2):147

[32] Buhry L, Azizi AH, Cheng S. Reactivation, replay, and preplay: How it might all fit together. Neuroscience. 2006;**31**(3):551-570

[33] Csikszentmihalyi M, Abuhamdeh S, Nakamura J. Flow. In: Elliot AJ, Dweck CS, editors. Handbook of Competence and Motivation. The Guilford Press. 1990. pp. 598-608